C-674  CAREER EXAMINATION SERIES

*This is your*
*PASSBOOK for...*

# Research Assistant

*Test Preparation Study Guide*
*Questions & Answers*

# COPYRIGHT NOTICE

This book is SOLELY intended for, is sold ONLY to, and its use is RESTRICTED to individual, bona fide applicants or candidates who qualify by virtue of having seriously filed applications for appropriate license, certificate, professional and/or promotional advancement, higher school matriculation, scholarship, or other legitimate requirements of education and/or governmental authorities.

This book is NOT intended for use, class instruction, tutoring, training, duplication, copying, reprinting, excerption, or adaptation, etc., by:

1) Other publishers
2) Proprietors and/or Instructors of "Coaching" and/or Preparatory Courses
3) Personnel and/or Training Divisions of commercial, industrial, and governmental organizations
4) Schools, colleges, or universities and/or their departments and staffs, including teachers and other personnel
5) Testing Agencies or Bureaus
6) Study groups which seek by the purchase of a single volume to copy and/or duplicate and/or adapt this material for use by the group as a whole without having purchased individual volumes for each of the members of the group
7) Et al.

Such persons would be in violation of appropriate Federal and State statutes.

PROVISION OF LICENSING AGREEMENTS – Recognized educational, commercial, industrial, and governmental institutions and organizations, and others legitimately engaged in educational pursuits, including training, testing, and measurement activities, may address request for a licensing agreement to the copyright owners, who will determine whether, and under what conditions, including fees and charges, the materials in this book may be used them. In other words, a licensing facility exists for the legitimate use of the material in this book on other than an individual basis. However, it is asseverated and affirmed here that the material in this book CANNOT be used without the receipt of the express permission of such a licensing agreement from the Publishers. Inquiries re licensing should be addressed to the company, attention rights and permissions department.

All rights reserved, including the right of reproduction in whole or in part, in any form or by any means, electronic or mechanical, including photocopying, recording, or by any information storage and retrieval system, without permission in writing from the Publisher.

Copyright © 2025 by
## National Learning Corporation

212 Michael Drive, Syosset, NY 11791
(516) 921-8888 • www.passbooks.com
E-mail: info@passbooks.com

# PASSBOOK® SERIES

THE *PASSBOOK® SERIES* has been created to prepare applicants and candidates for the ultimate academic battlefield – the examination room.

At some time in our lives, each and every one of us may be required to take an examination – for validation, matriculation, admission, qualification, registration, certification, or licensure.

Based on the assumption that every applicant or candidate has met the basic formal educational standards, has taken the required number of courses, and read the necessary texts, the *PASSBOOK® SERIES* furnishes the one special preparation which may assure passing with confidence, instead of failing with insecurity. Examination questions – together with answers – are furnished as the basic vehicle for study so that the mysteries of the examination and its compounding difficulties may be eliminated or diminished by a sure method.

This book is meant to help you pass your examination provided that you qualify and are serious in your objective.

The entire field is reviewed through the huge store of content information which is succinctly presented through a provocative and challenging approach – the question-and-answer method.

A climate of success is established by furnishing the correct answers at the end of each test.

You soon learn to recognize types of questions, forms of questions, and patterns of questioning. You may even begin to anticipate expected outcomes.

You perceive that many questions are repeated or adapted so that you can gain acute insights, which may enable you to score many sure points.

You learn how to confront new questions, or types of questions, and to attack them confidently and work out the correct answers.

You note objectives and emphases, and recognize pitfalls and dangers, so that you may make positive educational adjustments.

Moreover, you are kept fully informed in relation to new concepts, methods, practices, and directions in the field.

You discover that you are actually taking the examination all the time: you are preparing for the examination by "taking" an examination, not by reading extraneous and/or supererogatory textbooks.

In short, this PASSBOOK®, used directedly, should be an important factor in helping you to pass your test.

# RESEARCH ASSISTANT

DUTIES

Research Assistants, under general supervision, conduct research activities, special studies and writing assignments of more than ordinary difficulty and responsibility; perform research activities by collecting information and data of current and historical nature for use in the preparation of reports; obtain source materials by means of library research, examination of records, published materials or personal interviews; prepare written reports; maintain records of factual and statistical information; handle telephone and correspondence requests for information requiring research; perform quantitative analysis and prepare reports. Perform related work.

SCOPE OF THE EXAMINATION
The multiple-choice written test will cover knowledge, skills, and/or abilities in such areas as:

1. Information Ordering: The ability to follow correctly a rule or set of rules or actions in a certain order. The rule or set of rules used must be given. The things or actions to be put in order can include numbers, letters, words, pictures, procedures, sentences and mathematical or logical operations. Example: determine the logical order to complete tasks;
2. Matching: The degree to which one can compare letters, numbers, objects, pictures or patterns accurately. Example: compare two sources of information to detect errors;
3. Number Facility: The degree to which adding, subtracting, multiplying, dividing & finding percentages can be done quickly & correctly. Example: calculate the average numbers of hours worked by staff;
4. Written Expression: The ability to use English words or sentences in writing so that others will understand. Example: write well-written and accurate memos or reports; and
5. Deductive Reasoning: The ability to apply general rules to specific problems to come up with logical answers. Example: locate information in a policy that applies to employees.

# HOW TO TAKE A TEST

I. YOU MUST PASS AN EXAMINATION

A. *WHAT EVERY CANDIDATE SHOULD KNOW*

Examination applicants often ask us for help in preparing for the written test. What can I study in advance? What kinds of questions will be asked? How will the test be given? How will the papers be graded?

As an applicant for a civil service examination, you may be wondering about some of these things. Our purpose here is to suggest effective methods of advance study and to describe civil service examinations.

Your chances for success on this examination can be increased if you know how to prepare. Those "pre-examination jitters" can be reduced if you know what to expect. You can even experience an adventure in good citizenship if you know why civil service exams are given.

B. *WHY ARE CIVIL SERVICE EXAMINATIONS GIVEN?*

Civil service examinations are important to you in two ways. As a citizen, you want public jobs filled by employees who know how to do their work. As a job seeker, you want a fair chance to compete for that job on an equal footing with other candidates. The best-known means of accomplishing this two-fold goal is the competitive examination.

Exams are widely publicized throughout the nation. They may be administered for jobs in federal, state, city, municipal, town or village governments or agencies.

Any citizen may apply, with some limitations, such as the age or residence of applicants. Your experience and education may be reviewed to see whether you meet the requirements for the particular examination. When these requirements exist, they are reasonable and applied consistently to all applicants. Thus, a competitive examination may cause you some uneasiness now, but it is your privilege and safeguard.

C. *HOW ARE CIVIL SERVICE EXAMS DEVELOPED?*

Examinations are carefully written by trained technicians who are specialists in the field known as "psychological measurement," in consultation with recognized authorities in the field of work that the test will cover. These experts recommend the subject matter areas or skills to be tested; only those knowledges or skills important to your success on the job are included. The most reliable books and source materials available are used as references. Together, the experts and technicians judge the difficulty level of the questions.

Test technicians know how to phrase questions so that the problem is clearly stated. Their ethics do not permit "trick" or "catch" questions. Questions may have been tried out on sample groups, or subjected to statistical analysis, to determine their usefulness.

Written tests are often used in combination with performance tests, ratings of training and experience, and oral interviews. All of these measures combine to form the best-known means of finding the right person for the right job.

## II. HOW TO PASS THE WRITTEN TEST

### A. NATURE OF THE EXAMINATION

To prepare intelligently for civil service examinations, you should know how they differ from school examinations you have taken. In school you were assigned certain definite pages to read or subjects to cover. The examination questions were quite detailed and usually emphasized memory. Civil service exams, on the other hand, try to discover your present ability to perform the duties of a position, plus your potentiality to learn these duties. In other words, a civil service exam attempts to predict how successful you will be. Questions cover such a broad area that they cannot be as minute and detailed as school exam questions.

In the public service similar kinds of work, or positions, are grouped together in one "class." This process is known as *position-classification*. All the positions in a class are paid according to the salary range for that class. One class title covers all of these positions, and they are all tested by the same examination.

### B. FOUR BASIC STEPS

#### 1) Study the announcement

How, then, can you know what subjects to study? Our best answer is: "Learn as much as possible about the class of positions for which you've applied." The exam will test the knowledge, skills and abilities needed to do the work.

Your most valuable source of information about the position you want is the official exam announcement. This announcement lists the training and experience qualifications. Check these standards and apply only if you come reasonably close to meeting them.

The brief description of the position in the examination announcement offers some clues to the subjects which will be tested. Think about the job itself. Review the duties in your mind. Can you perform them, or are there some in which you are rusty? Fill in the blank spots in your preparation.

Many jurisdictions preview the written test in the exam announcement by including a section called "Knowledge and Abilities Required," "Scope of the Examination," or some similar heading. Here you will find out specifically what fields will be tested.

#### 2) Review your own background

Once you learn in general what the position is all about, and what you need to know to do the work, ask yourself which subjects you already know fairly well and which need improvement. You may wonder whether to concentrate on improving your strong areas or on building some background in your fields of weakness. When the announcement has specified "some knowledge" or "considerable knowledge," or has used adjectives like "beginning principles of…" or "advanced … methods," you can get a clue as to the number and difficulty of questions to be asked in any given field. More questions, and hence broader coverage, would be included for those subjects which are more important in the work. Now weigh your strengths and weaknesses against the job requirements and prepare accordingly.

#### 3) Determine the level of the position

Another way to tell how intensively you should prepare is to understand the level of the job for which you are applying. Is it the entering level? In other words, is this the position in which beginners in a field of work are hired? Or is it an intermediate or advanced level? Sometimes this is indicated by such words as "Junior" or "Senior" in the class title. Other jurisdictions use Roman numerals to designate the level – Clerk I, Clerk II, for example. The word "Supervisor" sometimes appears in the title. If the level is not indicated by the title, check the description of duties. Will you be working under very close supervision, or will you have responsibility for independent decisions in this work?

**4) Choose appropriate study materials**

Now that you know the subjects to be examined and the relative amount of each subject to be covered, you can choose suitable study materials. For beginning level jobs, or even advanced ones, if you have a pronounced weakness in some aspect of your training, read a modern, standard textbook in that field. Be sure it is up to date and has general coverage. Such books are normally available at your library, and the librarian will be glad to help you locate one. For entry-level positions, questions of appropriate difficulty are chosen – neither highly advanced questions, nor those too simple. Such questions require careful thought but not advanced training.

If the position for which you are applying is technical or advanced, you will read more advanced, specialized material. If you are already familiar with the basic principles of your field, elementary textbooks would waste your time. Concentrate on advanced textbooks and technical periodicals. Think through the concepts and review difficult problems in your field.

These are all general sources. You can get more ideas on your own initiative, following these leads. For example, training manuals and publications of the government agency which employs workers in your field can be useful, particularly for technical and professional positions. A letter or visit to the government department involved may result in more specific study suggestions, and certainly will provide you with a more definite idea of the exact nature of the position you are seeking.

## III. KINDS OF TESTS

Tests are used for purposes other than measuring knowledge and ability to perform specified duties. For some positions, it is equally important to test ability to make adjustments to new situations or to profit from training. In others, basic mental abilities not dependent on information are essential. Questions which test these things may not appear as pertinent to the duties of the position as those which test for knowledge and information. Yet they are often highly important parts of a fair examination. For very general questions, it is almost impossible to help you direct your study efforts. What we can do is to point out some of the more common of these general abilities needed in public service positions and describe some typical questions.

1) General information

Broad, general information has been found useful for predicting job success in some kinds of work. This is tested in a variety of ways, from vocabulary lists to questions about current events. Basic background in some field of work, such as sociology or economics, may be sampled in a group of questions. Often these are principles which have become familiar to most persons through exposure rather than through formal training. It is difficult to advise you how to study for these questions; being alert to the world around you is our best suggestion.

2) Verbal ability

An example of an ability needed in many positions is verbal or language ability. Verbal ability is, in brief, the ability to use and understand words. Vocabulary and grammar tests are typical measures of this ability. Reading comprehension or paragraph interpretation questions are common in many kinds of civil service tests. You are given a paragraph of written material and asked to find its central meaning.

3) Numerical ability
   Number skills can be tested by the familiar arithmetic problem, by checking paired lists of numbers to see which are alike and which are different, or by interpreting charts and graphs. In the latter test, a graph may be printed in the test booklet which you are asked to use as the basis for answering questions.

4) Observation
   A popular test for law-enforcement positions is the observation test. A picture is shown to you for several minutes, then taken away. Questions about the picture test your ability to observe both details and larger elements.

5) Following directions
   In many positions in the public service, the employee must be able to carry out written instructions dependably and accurately. You may be given a chart with several columns, each column listing a variety of information. The questions require you to carry out directions involving the information given in the chart.

6) Skills and aptitudes
   Performance tests effectively measure some manual skills and aptitudes. When the skill is one in which you are trained, such as typing or shorthand, you can practice. These tests are often very much like those given in business school or high school courses. For many of the other skills and aptitudes, however, no short-time preparation can be made. Skills and abilities natural to you or that you have developed throughout your lifetime are being tested.

   Many of the general questions just described provide all the data needed to answer the questions and ask you to use your reasoning ability to find the answers. Your best preparation for these tests, as well as for tests of facts and ideas, is to be at your physical and mental best. You, no doubt, have your own methods of getting into an exam-taking mood and keeping "in shape." The next section lists some ideas on this subject.

## IV. KINDS OF QUESTIONS

Only rarely is the "essay" question, which you answer in narrative form, used in civil service tests. Civil service tests are usually of the short-answer type. Full instructions for answering these questions will be given to you at the examination. But in case this is your first experience with short-answer questions and separate answer sheets, here is what you need to know:

### 1) Multiple-choice Questions
Most popular of the short-answer questions is the "multiple choice" or "best answer" question. It can be used, for example, to test for factual knowledge, ability to solve problems or judgment in meeting situations found at work.
   A multiple-choice question is normally one of three types—
- It can begin with an incomplete statement followed by several possible endings. You are to find the one ending which *best* completes the statement, although some of the others may not be entirely wrong.
- It can also be a complete statement in the form of a question which is answered by choosing one of the statements listed.

- It can be in the form of a problem – again you select the best answer.

Here is an example of a multiple-choice question with a discussion which should give you some clues as to the method for choosing the right answer:

When an employee has a complaint about his assignment, the action which will *best* help him overcome his difficulty is to
- A. discuss his difficulty with his coworkers
- B. take the problem to the head of the organization
- C. take the problem to the person who gave him the assignment
- D. say nothing to anyone about his complaint

In answering this question, you should study each of the choices to find which is best. Consider choice "A" – Certainly an employee may discuss his complaint with fellow employees, but no change or improvement can result, and the complaint remains unresolved. Choice "B" is a poor choice since the head of the organization probably does not know what assignment you have been given, and taking your problem to him is known as "going over the head" of the supervisor. The supervisor, or person who made the assignment, is the person who can clarify it or correct any injustice. Choice "C" is, therefore, correct. To say nothing, as in choice "D," is unwise. Supervisors have and interest in knowing the problems employees are facing, and the employee is seeking a solution to his problem.

## 2) True/False Questions

The "true/false" or "right/wrong" form of question is sometimes used. Here a complete statement is given. Your job is to decide whether the statement is right or wrong.

SAMPLE: A roaming cell-phone call to a nearby city costs less than a non-roaming call to a distant city.

This statement is wrong, or false, since roaming calls are more expensive.

This is not a complete list of all possible question forms, although most of the others are variations of these common types. You will always get complete directions for answering questions. Be sure you understand *how* to mark your answers – ask questions until you do.

## V. RECORDING YOUR ANSWERS

Computer terminals are used more and more today for many different kinds of exams.
For an examination with very few applicants, you may be told to record your answers in the test booklet itself. Separate answer sheets are much more common. If this separate answer sheet is to be scored by machine – and this is often the case – it is highly important that you mark your answers correctly in order to get credit.
An electronic scoring machine is often used in civil service offices because of the speed with which papers can be scored. Machine-scored answer sheets must be marked with a pencil, which will be given to you. This pencil has a high graphite content which responds to the electronic scoring machine. As a matter of fact, stray dots may register as answers, so do not let your pencil rest on the answer sheet while you are pondering the correct answer. Also, if your pencil lead breaks or is otherwise defective, ask for another.

Since the answer sheet will be dropped in a slot in the scoring machine, be careful not to bend the corners or get the paper crumpled.

The answer sheet normally has five vertical columns of numbers, with 30 numbers to a column. These numbers correspond to the question numbers in your test booklet. After each number, going across the page are four or five pairs of dotted lines. These short dotted lines have small letters or numbers above them. The first two pairs may also have a "T" or "F" above the letters. This indicates that the first two pairs only are to be used if the questions are of the true-false type. If the questions are multiple choice, disregard the "T" and "F" and pay attention only to the small letters or numbers.

Answer your questions in the manner of the sample that follows:

32. The largest city in the United States is
    A. Washington, D.C.
    B. New York City
    C. Chicago
    D. Detroit
    E. San Francisco

1) Choose the answer you think is best. (New York City is the largest, so "B" is correct.)
2) Find the row of dotted lines numbered the same as the question you are answering. (Find row number 32)
3) Find the pair of dotted lines corresponding to the answer. (Find the pair of lines under the mark "B.")
4) Make a solid black mark between the dotted lines.


## VI. BEFORE THE TEST

Common sense will help you find procedures to follow to get ready for an examination. Too many of us, however, overlook these sensible measures. Indeed, nervousness and fatigue have been found to be the most serious reasons why applicants fail to do their best on civil service tests. Here is a list of reminders:

- Begin your preparation early – Don't wait until the last minute to go scurrying around for books and materials or to find out what the position is all about.
- Prepare continuously – An hour a night for a week is better than an all-night cram session. This has been definitely established. What is more, a night a week for a month will return better dividends than crowding your study into a shorter period of time.
- Locate the place of the exam – You have been sent a notice telling you when and where to report for the examination. If the location is in a different town or otherwise unfamiliar to you, it would be well to inquire the best route and learn something about the building.
- Relax the night before the test – Allow your mind to rest. Do not study at all that night. Plan some mild recreation or diversion; then go to bed early and get a good night's sleep.
- Get up early enough to make a leisurely trip to the place for the test – This way unforeseen events, traffic snarls, unfamiliar buildings, etc. will not upset you.
- Dress comfortably – A written test is not a fashion show. You will be known by number and not by name, so wear something comfortable.

- Leave excess paraphernalia at home – Shopping bags and odd bundles will get in your way. You need bring only the items mentioned in the official notice you received; usually everything you need is provided. Do not bring reference books to the exam. They will only confuse those last minutes and be taken away from you when in the test room.
- Arrive somewhat ahead of time – If because of transportation schedules you must get there very early, bring a newspaper or magazine to take your mind off yourself while waiting.
- Locate the examination room – When you have found the proper room, you will be directed to the seat or part of the room where you will sit. Sometimes you are given a sheet of instructions to read while you are waiting. Do not fill out any forms until you are told to do so; just read them and be prepared.
- Relax and prepare to listen to the instructions
- If you have any physical problem that may keep you from doing your best, be sure to tell the test administrator. If you are sick or in poor health, you really cannot do your best on the exam. You can come back and take the test some other time.

## VII. AT THE TEST

The day of the test is here and you have the test booklet in your hand. The temptation to get going is very strong. Caution! There is more to success than knowing the right answers. You must know how to identify your papers and understand variations in the type of short-answer question used in this particular examination. Follow these suggestions for maximum results from your efforts:

### 1) Cooperate with the monitor

The test administrator has a duty to create a situation in which you can be as much at ease as possible. He will give instructions, tell you when to begin, check to see that you are marking your answer sheet correctly, and so on. He is not there to guard you, although he will see that your competitors do not take unfair advantage. He wants to help you do your best.

### 2) Listen to all instructions

Don't jump the gun! Wait until you understand all directions. In most civil service tests you get more time than you need to answer the questions. So don't be in a hurry. Read each word of instructions until you clearly understand the meaning. Study the examples, listen to all announcements and follow directions. Ask questions if you do not understand what to do.

### 3) Identify your papers

Civil service exams are usually identified by number only. You will be assigned a number; you must not put your name on your test papers. Be sure to copy your number correctly. Since more than one exam may be given, copy your exact examination title.

### 4) Plan your time

Unless you are told that a test is a "speed" or "rate of work" test, speed itself is usually not important. Time enough to answer all the questions will be provided, but this does not mean that you have all day. An overall time limit has been set. Divide the total time (in minutes) by the number of questions to determine the approximate time you have for each question.

### 5) Do not linger over difficult questions

If you come across a difficult question, mark it with a paper clip (useful to have along) and come back to it when you have been through the booklet. One caution if you do this – be sure to skip a number on your answer sheet as well. Check often to be sure that you have not lost your place and that you are marking in the row numbered the same as the question you are answering.

### 6) Read the questions

Be sure you know what the question asks! Many capable people are unsuccessful because they failed to *read* the questions correctly.

### 7) Answer all questions

Unless you have been instructed that a penalty will be deducted for incorrect answers, it is better to guess than to omit a question.

### 8) Speed tests

It is often better NOT to guess on speed tests. It has been found that on timed tests people are tempted to spend the last few seconds before time is called in marking answers at random – without even reading them – in the hope of picking up a few extra points. To discourage this practice, the instructions may warn you that your score will be "corrected" for guessing. That is, a penalty will be applied. The incorrect answers will be deducted from the correct ones, or some other penalty formula will be used.

### 9) Review your answers

If you finish before time is called, go back to the questions you guessed or omitted to give them further thought. Review other answers if you have time.

### 10) Return your test materials

If you are ready to leave before others have finished or time is called, take ALL your materials to the monitor and leave quietly. Never take any test material with you. The monitor can discover whose papers are not complete, and taking a test booklet may be grounds for disqualification.

## VIII. EXAMINATION TECHNIQUES

1) Read the general instructions carefully. These are usually printed on the first page of the exam booklet. As a rule, these instructions refer to the timing of the examination; the fact that you should not start work until the signal and must stop work at a signal, etc. If there are any *special* instructions, such as a choice of questions to be answered, make sure that you note this instruction carefully.

2) When you are ready to start work on the examination, that is as soon as the signal has been given, read the instructions to each question booklet, underline any key words or phrases, such as *least, best, outline, describe* and the like. In this way you will tend to answer as requested rather than discover on reviewing your paper that you *listed without describing*, that you selected the *worst* choice rather than the *best* choice, etc.

3) If the examination is of the objective or multiple-choice type – that is, each question will also give a series of possible answers: A, B, C or D, and you are called upon to select the best answer and write the letter next to that answer on your answer paper – it is advisable to start answering each question in turn. There may be anywhere from 50 to 100 such questions in the three or four hours allotted and you can see how much time would be taken if you read through all the questions before beginning to answer any. Furthermore, if you come across a question or group of questions which you know would be difficult to answer, it would undoubtedly affect your handling of all the other questions.

4) If the examination is of the essay type and contains but a few questions, it is a moot point as to whether you should read all the questions before starting to answer any one. Of course, if you are given a choice – say five out of seven and the like – then it is essential to read all the questions so you can eliminate the two that are most difficult. If, however, you are asked to answer all the questions, there may be danger in trying to answer the easiest one first because you may find that you will spend too much time on it. The best technique is to answer the first question, then proceed to the second, etc.

5) Time your answers. Before the exam begins, write down the time it started, then add the time allowed for the examination and write down the time it must be completed, then divide the time available somewhat as follows:
   - If 3-1/2 hours are allowed, that would be 210 minutes. If you have 80 objective-type questions, that would be an average of 2-1/2 minutes per question. Allow yourself no more than 2 minutes per question, or a total of 160 minutes, which will permit about 50 minutes to review.
   - If for the time allotment of 210 minutes there are 7 essay questions to answer, that would average about 30 minutes a question. Give yourself only 25 minutes per question so that you have about 35 minutes to review.

6) The most important instruction is to *read each question* and make sure you know what is wanted. The second most important instruction is to *time yourself properly* so that you answer every question. The third most important instruction is to *answer every question*. Guess if you have to but include something for each question. Remember that you will receive no credit for a blank and will probably receive some credit if you write something in answer to an essay question. If you guess a letter – say "B" for a multiple-choice question – you may have guessed right. If you leave a blank as an answer to a multiple-choice question, the examiners may respect your feelings but it will not add a point to your score. Some exams may penalize you for wrong answers, so in such cases *only*, you may not want to guess unless you have some basis for your answer.

7) Suggestions
   a. Objective-type questions
      1. Examine the question booklet for proper sequence of pages and questions
      2. Read all instructions carefully
      3. Skip any question which seems too difficult; return to it after all other questions have been answered
      4. Apportion your time properly; do not spend too much time on any single question or group of questions

5. Note and underline key words – *all, most, fewest, least, best, worst, same, opposite,* etc.
6. Pay particular attention to negatives
7. Note unusual option, e.g., unduly long, short, complex, different or similar in content to the body of the question
8. Observe the use of "hedging" words – *probably, may, most likely,* etc.
9. Make sure that your answer is put next to the same number as the question
10. Do not second-guess unless you have good reason to believe the second answer is definitely more correct
11. Cross out original answer if you decide another answer is more accurate; do not erase until you are ready to hand your paper in
12. Answer all questions; guess unless instructed otherwise
13. Leave time for review

  b. Essay questions
1. Read each question carefully
2. Determine exactly what is wanted. Underline key words or phrases.
3. Decide on outline or paragraph answer
4. Include many different points and elements unless asked to develop any one or two points or elements
5. Show impartiality by giving pros and cons unless directed to select one side only
6. Make and write down any assumptions you find necessary to answer the questions
7. Watch your English, grammar, punctuation and choice of words
8. Time your answers; don't crowd material

8) Answering the essay question

Most essay questions can be answered by framing the specific response around several key words or ideas. Here are a few such key words or ideas:

M's: manpower, materials, methods, money, management
P's: purpose, program, policy, plan, procedure, practice, problems, pitfalls, personnel, public relations

  a. Six basic steps in handling problems:
1. Preliminary plan and background development
2. Collect information, data and facts
3. Analyze and interpret information, data and facts
4. Analyze and develop solutions as well as make recommendations
5. Prepare report and sell recommendations
6. Install recommendations and follow up effectiveness

  b. Pitfalls to avoid
1. *Taking things for granted* – A statement of the situation does not necessarily imply that each of the elements is necessarily true; for example, a complaint may be invalid and biased so that all that can be taken for granted is that a complaint has been registered

2. *Considering only one side of a situation* – Wherever possible, indicate several alternatives and then point out the reasons you selected the best one
3. *Failing to indicate follow up* – Whenever your answer indicates action on your part, make certain that you will take proper follow-up action to see how successful your recommendations, procedures or actions turn out to be
4. *Taking too long in answering any single question* – Remember to time your answers properly

## IX. AFTER THE TEST

Scoring procedures differ in detail among civil service jurisdictions although the general principles are the same. Whether the papers are hand-scored or graded by machine we have described, they are nearly always graded by number. That is, the person who marks the paper knows only the number – never the name – of the applicant. Not until all the papers have been graded will they be matched with names. If other tests, such as training and experience or oral interview ratings have been given, scores will be combined. Different parts of the examination usually have different weights. For example, the written test might count 60 percent of the final grade, and a rating of training and experience 40 percent. In many jurisdictions, veterans will have a certain number of points added to their grades.

After the final grade has been determined, the names are placed in grade order and an eligible list is established. There are various methods for resolving ties between those who get the same final grade – probably the most common is to place first the name of the person whose application was received first. Job offers are made from the eligible list in the order the names appear on it. You will be notified of your grade and your rank as soon as all these computations have been made. This will be done as rapidly as possible.

People who are found to meet the requirements in the announcement are called "eligibles." Their names are put on a list of eligible candidates. An eligible's chances of getting a job depend on how high he stands on this list and how fast agencies are filling jobs from the list.

When a job is to be filled from a list of eligibles, the agency asks for the names of people on the list of eligibles for that job. When the civil service commission receives this request, it sends to the agency the names of the three people highest on this list. Or, if the job to be filled has specialized requirements, the office sends the agency the names of the top three persons who meet these requirements from the general list.

The appointing officer makes a choice from among the three people whose names were sent to him. If the selected person accepts the appointment, the names of the others are put back on the list to be considered for future openings.

That is the rule in hiring from all kinds of eligible lists, whether they are for typist, carpenter, chemist, or something else. For every vacancy, the appointing officer has his choice of any one of the top three eligibles on the list. This explains why the person whose name is on top of the list sometimes does not get an appointment when some of the persons lower on the list do. If the appointing officer chooses the second or third eligible, the No. 1 eligible does not get a job at once, but stays on the list until he is appointed or the list is terminated.

# X. HOW TO PASS THE INTERVIEW TEST

The examination for which you applied requires an oral interview test. You have already taken the written test and you are now being called for the interview test – the final part of the formal examination.

You may think that it is not possible to prepare for an interview test and that there are no procedures to follow during an interview. Our purpose is to point out some things you can do in advance that will help you and some good rules to follow and pitfalls to avoid while you are being interviewed.

*What is an interview supposed to test?*

The written examination is designed to test the technical knowledge and competence of the candidate; the oral is designed to evaluate intangible qualities, not readily measured otherwise, and to establish a list showing the relative fitness of each candidate – as measured against his competitors – for the position sought. Scoring is not on the basis of "right" and "wrong," but on a sliding scale of values ranging from "not passable" to "outstanding." As a matter of fact, it is possible to achieve a relatively low score without a single "incorrect" answer because of evident weakness in the qualities being measured.

Occasionally, an examination may consist entirely of an oral test – either an individual or a group oral. In such cases, information is sought concerning the technical knowledges and abilities of the candidate, since there has been no written examination for this purpose. More commonly, however, an oral test is used to supplement a written examination.

*Who conducts interviews?*

The composition of oral boards varies among different jurisdictions. In nearly all, a representative of the personnel department serves as chairman. One of the members of the board may be a representative of the department in which the candidate would work. In some cases, "outside experts" are used, and, frequently, a businessman or some other representative of the general public is asked to serve. Labor and management or other special groups may be represented. The aim is to secure the services of experts in the appropriate field.

However the board is composed, it is a good idea (and not at all improper or unethical) to ascertain in advance of the interview who the members are and what groups they represent. When you are introduced to them, you will have some idea of their backgrounds and interests, and at least you will not stutter and stammer over their names.

*What should be done before the interview?*

While knowledge about the board members is useful and takes some of the surprise element out of the interview, there is other preparation which is more substantive. It *is* possible to prepare for an oral interview – in several ways:

**1) Keep a copy of your application and review it carefully before the interview**

This may be the only document before the oral board, and the starting point of the interview. Know what education and experience you have listed there, and the sequence and dates of all of it. Sometimes the board will ask you to review the highlights of your experience for them; you should not have to hem and haw doing it.

**2) Study the class specification and the examination announcement**

Usually, the oral board has one or both of these to guide them. The qualities, characteristics or knowledges required by the position sought are stated in these documents. They offer valuable clues as to the nature of the oral interview. For example, if the job involves supervisory responsibilities, the announcement will usually indicate that knowledge of modern supervisory methods and the qualifications of the candidate as a supervisor will be tested. If so, you can expect such questions, frequently in the form of a hypothetical situation which you are expected to solve. NEVER go into an oral without knowledge of the duties and responsibilities of the job you seek.

### 3) Think through each qualification required

Try to visualize the kind of questions you would ask if you were a board member. How well could you answer them? Try especially to appraise your own knowledge and background in each area, *measured against the job sought*, and identify any areas in which you are weak. Be critical and realistic – do not flatter yourself.

### 4) Do some general reading in areas in which you feel you may be weak

For example, if the job involves supervision and your past experience has NOT, some general reading in supervisory methods and practices, particularly in the field of human relations, might be useful. Do NOT study agency procedures or detailed manuals. The oral board will be testing your understanding and capacity, not your memory.

### 5) Get a good night's sleep and watch your general health and mental attitude

You will want a clear head at the interview. Take care of a cold or any other minor ailment, and of course, no hangovers.

*What should be done on the day of the interview?*

Now comes the day of the interview itself. Give yourself plenty of time to get there. Plan to arrive somewhat ahead of the scheduled time, particularly if your appointment is in the fore part of the day. If a previous candidate fails to appear, the board might be ready for you a bit early. By early afternoon an oral board is almost invariably behind schedule if there are many candidates, and you may have to wait. Take along a book or magazine to read, or your application to review, but leave any extraneous material in the waiting room when you go in for your interview. In any event, relax and compose yourself.

The matter of dress is important. The board is forming impressions about you – from your experience, your manners, your attitude, and your appearance. Give your personal appearance careful attention. Dress your best, but not your flashiest. Choose conservative, appropriate clothing, and be sure it is immaculate. This is a business interview, and your appearance should indicate that you regard it as such. Besides, being well groomed and properly dressed will help boost your confidence.

Sooner or later, someone will call your name and escort you into the interview room. *This is it.* From here on you are on your own. It is too late for any more preparation. But remember, you asked for this opportunity to prove your fitness, and you are here because your request was granted.

*What happens when you go in?*

The usual sequence of events will be as follows: The clerk (who is often the board stenographer) will introduce you to the chairman of the oral board, who will introduce you to the other members of the board. Acknowledge the introductions before you sit down. Do not be surprised if you find a microphone facing you or a stenotypist sitting by. Oral interviews are usually recorded in the event of an appeal or other review.

Usually the chairman of the board will open the interview by reviewing the highlights of your education and work experience from your application – primarily for the benefit of the other members of the board, as well as to get the material into the record. Do not interrupt or comment unless there is an error or significant misinterpretation; if that is the case, do not hesitate. But do not quibble about insignificant matters. Also, he will usually ask you some question about your education, experience or your present job – partly to get you to start talking and to establish the interviewing "rapport." He may start the actual questioning, or turn it over to one of the other members. Frequently, each member undertakes the questioning on a particular area, one in which he is perhaps most competent, so you can expect each member to participate in the examination. Because time is limited, you may also expect some rather abrupt switches in the direction the questioning takes, so do not be upset by it. Normally, a board member will not pursue a single line of questioning unless he discovers a particular strength or weakness.

After each member has participated, the chairman will usually ask whether any member has any further questions, then will ask you if you have anything you wish to add. Unless you are expecting this question, it may floor you. Worse, it may start you off on an extended, extemporaneous speech. The board is not usually seeking more information. The question is principally to offer you a last opportunity to present further qualifications or to indicate that you have nothing to add. So, if you feel that a significant qualification or characteristic has been overlooked, it is proper to point it out in a sentence or so. Do not compliment the board on the thoroughness of their examination – they have been sketchy, and you know it. If you wish, merely say, "No thank you, I have nothing further to add." This is a point where you can "talk yourself out" of a good impression or fail to present an important bit of information. Remember, *you close the interview yourself.*

The chairman will then say, "That is all, Mr. _____, thank you." Do not be startled; the interview is over, and quicker than you think. Thank him, gather your belongings and take your leave. Save your sigh of relief for the other side of the door.


*How to put your best foot forward*

Throughout this entire process, you may feel that the board individually and collectively is trying to pierce your defenses, seek out your hidden weaknesses and embarrass and confuse you. Actually, this is not true. They are obliged to make an appraisal of your qualifications for the job you are seeking, and they want to see you in your best light. Remember, they must interview all candidates and a non-cooperative candidate may become a failure in spite of their best efforts to bring out his qualifications. Here are 15 suggestions that will help you:

### 1) Be natural – Keep your attitude confident, not cocky

If you are not confident that you can do the job, do not expect the board to be. Do not apologize for your weaknesses, try to bring out your strong points. The board is interested in a positive, not negative, presentation. Cockiness will antagonize any board member and make him wonder if you are covering up a weakness by a false show of strength.

### 2) Get comfortable, but don't lounge or sprawl

Sit erectly but not stiffly. A careless posture may lead the board to conclude that you are careless in other things, or at least that you are not impressed by the importance of the occasion. Either conclusion is natural, even if incorrect. Do not fuss with your clothing, a pencil or an ashtray. Your hands may occasionally be useful to emphasize a point; do not let them become a point of distraction.

### 3) Do not wisecrack or make small talk

This is a serious situation, and your attitude should show that you consider it as such. Further, the time of the board is limited – they do not want to waste it, and neither should you.

**4) Do not exaggerate your experience or abilities**

In the first place, from information in the application or other interviews and sources, the board may know more about you than you think. Secondly, you probably will not get away with it. An experienced board is rather adept at spotting such a situation, so do not take the chance.

**5) If you know a board member, do not make a point of it, yet do not hide it**

Certainly you are not fooling him, and probably not the other members of the board. Do not try to take advantage of your acquaintanceship – it will probably do you little good.

**6) Do not dominate the interview**

Let the board do that. They will give you the clues – do not assume that you have to do all the talking. Realize that the board has a number of questions to ask you, and do not try to take up all the interview time by showing off your extensive knowledge of the answer to the first one.

**7) Be attentive**

You only have 20 minutes or so, and you should keep your attention at its sharpest throughout. When a member is addressing a problem or question to you, give him your undivided attention. Address your reply principally to him, but do not exclude the other board members.

**8) Do not interrupt**

A board member may be stating a problem for you to analyze. He will ask you a question when the time comes. Let him state the problem, and wait for the question.

**9) Make sure you understand the question**

Do not try to answer until you are sure what the question is. If it is not clear, restate it in your own words or ask the board member to clarify it for you. However, do not haggle about minor elements.

**10) Reply promptly but not hastily**

A common entry on oral board rating sheets is "candidate responded readily," or "candidate hesitated in replies." Respond as promptly and quickly as you can, but do not jump to a hasty, ill-considered answer.

**11) Do not be peremptory in your answers**

A brief answer is proper – but do not fire your answer back. That is a losing game from your point of view. The board member can probably ask questions much faster than you can answer them.

**12) Do not try to create the answer you think the board member wants**

He is interested in what kind of mind you have and how it works – not in playing games. Furthermore, he can usually spot this practice and will actually grade you down on it.

**13) Do not switch sides in your reply merely to agree with a board member**

Frequently, a member will take a contrary position merely to draw you out and to see if you are willing and able to defend your point of view. Do not start a debate, yet do not surrender a good position. If a position is worth taking, it is worth defending.

### 14) Do not be afraid to admit an error in judgment if you are shown to be wrong

The board knows that you are forced to reply without any opportunity for careful consideration. Your answer may be demonstrably wrong. If so, admit it and get on with the interview.

### 15) Do not dwell at length on your present job

The opening question may relate to your present assignment. Answer the question but do not go into an extended discussion. You are being examined for a *new* job, not your present one. As a matter of fact, try to phrase ALL your answers in terms of the job for which you are being examined.

*Basis of Rating*

Probably you will forget most of these "do's" and "don'ts" when you walk into the oral interview room. Even remembering them all will not ensure you a passing grade. Perhaps you did not have the qualifications in the first place. But remembering them will help you to put your best foot forward, without treading on the toes of the board members.

Rumor and popular opinion to the contrary notwithstanding, an oral board wants you to make the best appearance possible. They know you are under pressure – but they also want to see how you respond to it as a guide to what your reaction would be under the pressures of the job you seek. They will be influenced by the degree of poise you display, the personal traits you show and the manner in which you respond.

ABOUT THIS BOOK

This book contains tests divided into Examination Sections. Go through each test, answering every question in the margin. We have also attached a sample answer sheet at the back of the book that can be removed and used. At the end of each test look at the answer key and check your answers. On the ones you got wrong, look at the right answer choice and learn. Do not fill in the answers first. Do not memorize the questions and answers, but understand the answer and principles involved. On your test, the questions will likely be different from the samples. Questions are changed and new ones added. If you understand these past questions you should have success with any changes that arise. Tests may consist of several types of questions. We have additional books on each subject should more study be advisable or necessary for you. Finally, the more you study, the better prepared you will be. This book is intended to be the last thing you study before you walk into the examination room. Prior study of relevant texts is also recommended. NLC publishes some of these in our Fundamental Series. Knowledge and good sense are important factors in passing your exam. Good luck also helps. So now study this Passbook, absorb the material contained within and take that knowledge into the examination. Then do your best to pass that exam.

# EXAMINATION SECTION

# READING COMPREHENSION
# UNDERSTANDING AND INTERPRETING WRITTEN MATERIAL
# EXAMINATION SECTION
# TEST 1

DIRECTIONS: Each question or incomplete statement is followed by several suggested answers or completions. Select the one that BEST answers the question or completes the statement. *PRINT THE LETTER OF THE CORRECT ANSWER IN THE SPACE AT THE RIGHT.*

Questions 1-3.

DIRECTIONS: Questions 1 through 3 are to be answered SOLELY on the basis of the following passage.

Every organization needs a systematic method of checking its operations as a means to increase efficiency and promote economy. Many successful private firms have instituted a system of audit or internal inspections to accomplish these ends. Law enforcement organizations, which have an extremely important service to *sell*, should be no less zealous in developing efficiency and economy in their operations. Periodic, organized, and systematic inspections are one means of promoting the achievement of these objectives. The necessity of an organized inspection system is perhaps greatest in those law enforcement groups which have grown to such a size that the principal officer can no longer personally supervise or be cognizant of every action taken. Smooth and effective operation demands that the head of the organization have at hand some tool with which he can study and enforce general policies and procedure and also direct compliance with day-to-day orders, most of which are put into execution outside his sight and hearing. A good inspection system can serve as that tool.

1. The central thought of the above passage is that a system of inspections within a police department
    A. is unnecessary for a department in which the principal officer can personally supervise all official actions taken
    B. should be instituted at the first indication that there is any deterioration in job performance by the force
    C. should be decentralized and administered by first-line supervisory officers
    D. is an important aid to the police administrator in the accomplishment of law enforcement objectives

1.____

2. The MOST accurate of the following statements concerning the need for an organized inspection system in a law enforcement organization is: It is
    A. never needed in an organization of small size where the principal officer can give personal supervision
    B. most needed where the size of the organization prevents direct supervision by the principal officer
    C. more needed in law enforcement organizations than in private firms
    D. especially needed in an organization about to embark upon a needed expansion of services

2.____

3. According to the above passage, the head of the police organization utilizes the internal inspection system    3.____
   A. as a tool which must be constantly re-examined in the light of changing demands for police service
   B. as an administrative technique to increase efficiency and promote economy
   C. by personally visiting those areas of police operation which are outside his sight and hearing
   D. to augment the control of local commanders over detailed field operations

Questions 4-10.

DIRECTIONS: Questions 4 through 10 are to be answered SOLELY on the basis of the following passage.

Job evaluation and job rating systems are intended to introduce scientific procedures. Any type of approach, when properly used, will give satisfactory results. The Point System, when properly validated by actual use, is more likely to be suitable for general use than the ranking system. In many aspects, the Factor Comparison Plan is a point system tied to money values. Of course, there may be another system that combines the ranking system with the point system, especially during the initial stages of the development of the program. After the program has been in use for some time, the tendency is to drop off the ranking phase and continue the use of the point system.

In the ranking system of rating of jobs, every job within the plant is arranged in some order, either from the one with the simplest qualifications to the one with maximum requirements, or in the reverse order. This system should be preceded by careful job analysis and the writing of accurate job descriptions before the rating process is undertaken. It is possible, of course, to take the jobs as they are found in the business enterprise and use the names as they are without any attempt at standardization, and merely rank them according to the general overall impression of the raters. Such a procedure is certain to fall short of what may reasonably be expected of job rating. Another procedure that is in reality merely a modification of the simple rating described above is to establish a series of grades or zones and arrange all he jobs in the plant into groups within these grades and zones. The practice in most common use is to arrange all the jobs in the plant according to their requirements by rating them and then to establish the classification or groups.

The actual ranking of jobs may be done by one individual, several individuals, or a committee. If several individuals are working independently on the task, it will usually be found that, in general, they agree but that their rankings vary in certain details. A conference between the individuals, with each person giving his reasons why he rated one way or another, usually produces agreement. The detailed job descriptions are particularly helpful when there is disagreement among raters as to the rating of certain jobs. It is not only possible but desirable to have workers participate in the construction of the job description and in rating the job.

4. The MAIN theme of this passage is    4.____
   A. the elimination of bias in job rating
   B. the rating of jobs by the ranking system
   C. the need or accuracy in allocating points in the point system
   D. pitfalls to avoid in selecting key jobs in the Factor Comparison Plan

5. The ranking system of rating jobs consists MAINLY of
   A. attaching a point value to each ratable factor of each job prior to establishing an equitable pay scale
   B. arranging every job in the organization in descending order and then following this up with a job analysis of the key jobs
   C. preparing accurate job descriptions after a job analysis and then arranging all jobs either in ascending or descending order based on job requirements
   D. arbitrarily establishing a hierarchy of job classes and grades and then fitting each job into a specific class and grade based on the opinions of unit supervisors

6. The above passage states that the system of classifying jobs MOST used in an organization is to
   A. organize all jobs in the organization in accordance with their requirements and then create categories or clusters of jobs
   B. classify all jobs in the organization according to the titles and rank by which they are currently known in the organization
   C. establish a pre-arranged series of grades or zones and then fit all jobs into one of the grades or zones
   D. determine the salary currently being paid for each job and then rank the jobs in order according to salary

7. According to the above passage, experience has shown that when a group of raters is assigned to the job evaluation task and each individual rates independently of the others, the raters GENERALLY
   A. *agree* with respect to all aspects of their rankings
   B. *disagree* with respect to all or nearly all aspects of the rankings
   C. *disagree* on overall ratings, but agree on specific rating factors
   D. *agree* on overall rankings, but have some variance in some details

8. The above passage states that the use of a detailed job description is of special value when
   A. employees of an organization have participated in the preliminary step involved in actual preparation of the job description
   B. labor representatives are not participating in ranking of the jobs
   C. an individual rater who is unsure of himself is ranking the jobs
   D. a group of raters is having difficulty reaching unanimity with respect to ranking a certain job

9. A comparison of the various rating systems as described in the above passage shows that
   A. the ranking system is not as appropriate for general use as a properly validated point system
   B. the point system is the same as the Factor Comparison Plan except that it places greater emphasis on money

C. no system is capable of combining the point system and the Factor Comparison Plan
D. the point system will be discontinued last when used in combination with the Factor comparison System

10. The above passage implies that the PRINCIPAL reason for creating job evaluation and rating systems was to help
    A. overcome union opposition to existing salary plans
    B. base wage determination on a more objective and orderly foundation
    C. eliminate personal bias on the part of the trained scientific job evaluators
    D. management determine if it was overpricing the various jobs in the organizational hierarchy

10._____

Questions 11-13.

DIRECTIONS: Questions 11 through 13 are to be answered SOLELY on the basis of the following passage.

The common sense character of the merit system seems so natural to most Americans that many people wonder why it should ever have been inoperative. After all, the American economic system, the most phenomenal the world has ever known, is also founded on a rugged selective process which emphasizes the personal qualities of capacity, industriousness, and productivity. The criteria may not have always been appropriate and competition has not always been fair, but competition there was, and the responsibilities and the rewards—with exceptions, of course—have gone to those who could measure up in terms of intelligence, knowledge, or perseverance. This has been true not only in the economic area, in the money-making process, but also in achievement in the professions and other walks of life.

11. According to the above passage, economic rewards in the United State have
    A. always been based on appropriate, fair criteria
    B. only recently been based on a competitive system
    C. not going to people who compete too ruggedly
    D. usually gone to those people with intelligence, knowledge, and perseverance

11._____

12. According to the above passage, a merit system is
    A. an unfair criterion on which to base rewards
    B. unnatural to anyone who is not American
    C. based only on common sense
    D. based on the same principles as the American economic system

12._____

13. According to the above passage, it is MOST accurate to say that
    A. the United States has always had a civil service merit system
    B. civil service employees are very rugged
    C. the American economic system has always been based on a merit objective
    D. competition is unique to the American way of life

13._____

Questions 14-15.

DIRECTIONS: Questions 14 and 15 are to be answered SOLELY on the basis of the following passage.

In-basket tests are often used to assess managerial potential. The exercise consists of a set of papers that would be likely to be found in the in-basket of an administrator or manager at any given time, and requires the individuals participating in the examination to indicate how they would dispose of each item found in the in-basket. In order to handle the in-basket effectively, they must successfully manage their time, refer and assign some work to subordinates, juggle potentially conflicting appointments and meetings, and arrange for follow-up of problems generated by the items in the in-basket. In other words, the in-basket test is attempting to evaluate the participants' abilities to organize their work, set priorities, delegate, control, and make decisions.

14. According to the above passage, to succeed in an in-basket test, an administrator must
    A. be able to read very quickly
    B. have a great deal of technical knowledge
    C. know when to delegate work
    D. arrange a lot of appointments and meetings

14.____

15. According to the above passage, all of the following abilities are indications of managerial potential EXCEPT the ability to
    A. organize and control
    B. manage time
    C. write effective reports
    D. make appropriate decisions

15.____

Questions 16-19.

DIRECTIONS: Questions 16 through 19 are to be answered SOLELY on the basis of the following passage.

A personnel researcher has at his disposal various approaches for obtaining information, analyzing it, and arriving at conclusions that have value in predicting and affecting the behavior of people at work. The type of method to be used depends on such factors as the nature of the research problem, the available data, and the attitudes of those people being studied to the various kinds of approaches. While the experimental approach, with its use of control groups, is the most refined type of study, there are others that are often found useful in personnel research. Surveys, in which the researcher obtains facts on a problem from a variety of sources, are employed in research on wages, fringe benefits, and labor relations. Historical studies are used to trace the development of problems in order to understand them better and to isolate possible causative factors. Case studies are generally developed to explore all the details of a particular problem that is representative of other similar problems. A researcher chooses the most appropriate form of study for the problem he is investigating. He should recognize, however, that the experimental method, commonly referred to as the scientific method, if used validly and reliably, gives the most conclusive results.

16. The above passage discusses several approaches used to obtain information  16.____
on particular problems.
Which of the following may be MOST reasonably concluded from the passage?
A(n)
    A. historical study cannot determine causative factors
    B. survey is often used in research on fringe benefits
    C. case study is usually used to explore a problem that is unique and unrelated to other problems
    D. experimental study is used when the scientific approach to a problem fails

17. According to the above passage, all of the following are factors that may  17.____
determine the type of approach a researcher uses EXCEPT
    A. the attitudes of people toward being used in control groups
    B. the number of available sources
    C. his desire to isolate possible causative factors
    D. the degree of accuracy he requires

18. The words *scientific method*, as used in the last sentence of the above passage,  18.____
refer to a type of study which, according to the above passage
    A. uses a variety of sources
    B. traces the development of problems
    C. uses control groups
    D. analyzes the details of a representative problem

19. Which of the following can be MOST reasonably concluded from the above  19.____
passage?
In obtaining and analyzing information on a particular problem, a researcher employs the method which is the
    A. most accurate
    B. most suitable
    C. least expensive
    D. least time-consuming

Questions 20-25.

DIRECTIONS: Questions 20 through 25 are to be answered SOLELY on the basis of the following passage.

The quality of the voice of a worker is an important factor in conveying to clients and co-workers his attitude and, to some degree, his character. The human voice, when not consciously disguised, may reflect a person's mood, temper, and personality. It has been shown in several experiments that certain character traits can be assessed with better than chance accuracy through listening to the voice of an unknown person who cannot be seen.

Since one of the objectives of the worker is to put clients at ease and to present an encouraging and comfortable atmosphere, a harsh, shrill, or loud voice could have a negative effect. A client who displays emotions of anger or resentment would probably be provoked even further by a caustic tone. In a face-to-face situation, an unpleasant voice may be compensated for, to some degree, by a concerned and kind facial expression. However, when one speaks on the telephone, the expression on one's face cannot be seen by the listener. A supervising clerk who wishes to represent himself effectively to clients should try to eliminate as many faults as possible in striving to develop desirable voice qualities.

20. If a worker uses a sarcastic tone while interviewing a resentful client, the client, according to the above passage, would MOST likely
    A. avoid the face-to-face problem
    B. be ashamed of his behavior
    C. become more resentful
    D. be provoked to violence

21. According to the passage, experiments comparing voice and character traits have demonstrated that
    A. prospects for improving an unpleasant voice through training are better than chance
    B. the voice can be altered to project many different psychological characteristics
    C. the quality of the human voice reveals more about the speaker than his words do
    D. the speaker's voice tells the hearer something about the speaker's personality

22. Which of the following, according to the above passage, is a person's voice MOST likely to reveal?
    His
    A. prejudices
    B. intelligence
    C. social awareness
    D. temperament

23. It may be MOST reasonably concluded from the above passage that an interested and sympathetic expression on the face of a worker
    A. may induce a client to feel certain he will receive welfare benefits
    B. will eliminate the need for pleasant vocal qualities in the interviewer
    C. may help to make up for an unpleasant voice in the interviewer
    D. is desirable as the interviewer speaks on the telephone to a client

24. Of the following, the MOST reasonable implication of the above paragraph is that a worker should, when speaking to a client, control and use his voice to
    A. simulate a feeling of interest in the problems of the client
    B. express his emotions directly and adequately
    C. help produce in the client a sense of comfort and security
    D. reflect his own true personality

25. It may be concluded from the above passage that the PARTICULAR reason for a worker to pay special attention to modulating her voice when talking on the phone to a client is that, during a telephone conversation
    A. there is a necessity to compensate for the way in which a telephone distorts the voice
    B. the voice of the worker is a reflection of her mood and character
    C. the client can react only on the basis of the voice and words she hears
    D. the client may have difficulty getting a clear understanding over the telephone

## KEY (CORRECT ANSWERS)

| | | | |
|---|---|---|---|
| 1. | D | 11. | D |
| 2. | B | 12. | D |
| 3. | B | 13. | C |
| 4. | B | 14. | C |
| 5. | C | 15. | C |
| 6. | A | 16. | B |
| 7. | D | 17. | D |
| 8. | D | 18. | C |
| 9. | A | 19. | B |
| 10. | B | 20. | C |

21. D
22. D
23. C
24. C
25. C

# TEST 2

DIRECTIONS: Each question or incomplete statement is followed by several suggested answers or completions. Select the one that BEST answers the question or completes the statement. *PRINT THE LETTER OF THE CORRECT ANSWER IN THE SPACE AT THE RIGHT.*

Questions 1-3.

DIRECTIONS: Questions 1 through 3 are to be answered SOLELY on the basis of the following paragraph.

Suppose you are given the job of printing, collating, and stapling 8,000 copies of a ten-page booklet as soon as possible. You have available one photo-offset machine, a collator with an automatic stapler, and the personnel to operate these machines. All will be available for however long the job takes to complete. The photo-offset machine prints 5,000 impressions an hour, and it takes about 15 minutes to set up a plate. The collator, including time for insertion of pages and stapling, can process about 2,000 booklets an hour. (Answers should be based on the assumption that there are no breakdowns or delays.)

1. Assuming that all the printing is finished before the collating is started, if the job is given to you late Monday and your section can begin work the next day and is able to devote seven hours a day, Monday through Friday, to the job until it is finished, what is the BEST estimate of when the job will be finished?
    A. Wednesday afternoon of the same week
    B. Thursday morning of the same week
    C. Friday morning of the same week
    D. Monday morning of the next week

1.____

2. An operator suggests to you that instead of completing all the printing and then beginning collating and stapling, you first print all the pages for 4,000 booklets, so that they can be collated and stapled while the last 4,000 pages are being printed.
If you accepted this suggestion, the job would be completed
    A. sooner but would require more man-hours
    B at the same time using either method
    C. later and would require more man-hours
    D. sooner but there would be more wear and tear on the plates

2.____

3. Assume that you have the same assignment and equipment as described above, but 16,000 copies of the booklet are needed instead of 8,000.
If you decided to print 8,000 complete booklets, then collate and staple them while you started printing the next 8,000 booklets, which of the following statements would MOST accurately describe the relationship between this new method and your original method of printing all the booklets at one time, and then collating and stapling them? The
    A. job would be completed at the same time regardless of the method used
    B. new method would result in the job's being completed 3½ hours earlier
    C. original method would result in the job's being completed an hour later
    D. new method would result in the job's being completed 1½ hours earlier

3.____

Questions 4-6.

DIRECTIONS: Questions 4 through 6 are to be answered SOLELY on the basis of the following passage.

When using words like company, association, council, committee, and board in place of the full official name, the writer should not capitalize these short forms unless he intends them to invoke the full force of the institution's authority. In legal contracts, in minutes, or in formal correspondence where one is speaking formally and officially on behalf of the company, the term Company is usually capitalized, but in ordinary usage, where it is not essential to load the short form with this significance, capitalization would be excessive. (Example: The company will have many good openings for graduates this June.)

The treatment recommended for short forms of place names is essentially the same as that recommended for short forms of organizational names. In general, we capitalize the full form but not the short form. If Park Avenue is referred to in one sentence, then the *avenue* is sufficient in subsequent references. The same is true with words like building, hotel, station, and airport, which are capitalized when part of a proper name changed (Pan Am Building, Hotel Plaza, Union Station, O'Hare Airport), but are simply lower-cased when replacing these specific names.

4. The above passage states that USUALLY the short forms of names of organizations
   A. and places should not be capitalized
   B. and places should be capitalized
   C. should not be capitalized, but the short forms of names of places should be capitalized
   D. should be capitalized, but the short forms of names of places should not be capitalized

5. The above passage states that in legal contracts, in minutes, and in formal correspondence, the short forms of names of organizations should
   A. usually not be capitalized       B. usually be capitalized
   C. usually not be used              D. never be used

6. It can be inferred from the above passage that decisions regarding when to capitalize certain words
   A. should be left to the discretion of the writer
   B. should be based on generally accepted rules
   C. depend on the total number of words capitalized
   D. are of minor importance

Questions 7-10.

DIRECTIONS: Questions 7 through 10 are to be answered SOLELY on the basis of the following passage.

Use of the systems and procedures approach to office management is revolutionizing the supervision of office work. This approach views an enterprise as an entity which seeks to fulfill definite objectives. Systems and procedures help to organize repetitive work into a routine, thus reducing the amount of decision making required for its accomplishment. As a result, employees are guided in their efforts and perform only necessary work. Supervisors are relieved of any details of execution and are free to attend to more important work. Establishing work guides which require that identical tasks be performed the same way each time permits standardization of forms, machine operations, work methods, and controls. This approach also reduces the probability of errors. Any error committed is usually discovered quickly because the incorrect work does not meet the requirement of the work guides. Errors are also reduced through work specialization, which allows each employee to become thoroughly proficient in a particular type of work. Such proficiency also tends to improve the morale of the employees.

7. The above passage states that the accuracy of an employee's work is INCREASED by
    A. using the work specialization approach
    B. employing a probability sample
    C. requiring him to shift at one time into different types of tasks
    D. having his supervisor check each detail of work execution

8. Of the following, which one BEST expresses the main theme of the above passage? The
    A. advantages and disadvantages of the systems and procedures approach to office management
    B. effectiveness of the systems and procedures approach to office management in developing skills
    C. systems and procedures approach to office management as it relates to office costs
    D. advantages of the systems and procedures approach to office management for supervisors and office workers

9. Work guides are LEAST likely to be used when
    A. standardized forms are used
    B. a particular office task is distinct and different from all others
    C. identical tasks are to be performed in identical ways
    D. similar work methods are expected from each employee

10. According to the above passage, when an employee makes a work error, it USUALLY
    A. is quickly corrected by the supervisor
    B. necessitates a change in the work guides
    C. can be detected quickly if work guides are in use
    D. increases the probability of further errors by that employee

Questions 11-12.

DIRECTIONS: Questions 11 and 12 are to be answered SOLELY on the basis of the following passage.

The coordination of the many activities of a large public agency is absolutely essential. Coordination, as an administrative principle, must be distinguished from and is independent of cooperation. Coordination can be of either the horizontal or the vertical type. In large organizations, the objectives of vertical coordination are achieved by the transmission of orders and statements of policy down through the various levels of authority. It is an accepted generalization that the more authoritarian the organization, the more easily may vertical coordination be accomplished. Horizontal coordination is arrived through staff work, administrative management, and conferences of administrators of equal rank. It is obvious that of the two types of coordination, the vertical kind is more important, for at best horizontal coordination only supplements the coordination effected up and down the line,

11. According to the above passage, the ease with which vertical coordination is achieved in a large agency depends upon
    A. the extent to which control is firmly exercised from above
    B. the objectives that have been established for the agency
    C. the importance attached by employees to the orders and statements of policy transmitted through the agency
    D. the cooperation obtained at the various levels of authority

12. According to the above passage,
    A. vertical coordination is dependent for its success upon horizontal coordination
    B. one type of coordination may work in opposition to the other
    C. similar methods may be used to achieve both types of coordination
    D. horizontal coordination is at most an addition to vertical coordination

Questions 13-17.

DIRECTIONS: Questions 13 through 17 are to be answered SOLELY on the basis of the following situation.

Assume that you are a newly appointed supervisor in the same unit in which you have been acting as a provisional for some time. You have in your unit the following workers:

WORKER I: He has always been an efficient worker. In a number of his cases, the clients have recently begun to complain that they cannot manage on the departmental budget.

WORKER II: He has been under selective supervision for some time as an experienced, competent worker. He now begins to be late for his supervisory conferences and to stress how much work he has to do.

WORKER III: He has been making considerable improvement in his ability to handle the details of his job. He now tells you, during an individual conference, that he does not need such close supervision and that he wants to operate more independently. He says that Worker II is always available when he needs a little information or help but, in general, he can manage very well by himself.

WORKER IV: He brings you a complex case for decision as to eligibility. Discussion of the case brings out the fact that he has failed to consider all the available resources adequately but has stressed the family's needs to include every extra item in the budget. This is the third case of a similar nature that his worker has brought to you recently. This worker and Worker I work in adjacent territory and are rather friendly.

In the following questions, select the option that describes the method of dealing with these workers that illustrate BEST supervisory practice.

13. With respect to supervision of Worker I, the assistant supervisor should
    A. discuss with the worker, in an individual conference, any problems that he may be having due to the increase in the cost of living
    B. plan a group conference for the unit around budgeting, as both Workers I and IV seem to be having budgetary difficulties
    C. discuss with Workers I and IV together the meaning of money as acceptance or rejection to the clients
    D. discuss with Worker I the budgetary data in each case in relation to each client's situation

13.____

14. With respect to supervision of Worker II, the supervisory should
    A. move slowly with this worker and give him time to learn that the supervisor's official appointment has not changed his attitudes or methods of supervision
    B. discuss the worker's change of attitude and asks him to analyze the reasons for his change in behavior
    C. take time to show the worker how he is avoiding his responsibility in the supervisor-worker relationship and that he is resisting supervision
    D. hold an evaluatory conference with the worker and show him how he is taking over responsibilities that are not his by providing supervision for Worker III

14.____

15. With respect to supervision of Worker III, the supervisor should discuss with this worker
    A. why he would rather have supervision from Worker II than from the supervisor
    B. the necessity for further improvement before he can go on selective supervision
    C. an analysis of the improvement that has been made and the extent to which the worker is able to handle the total job for which he is responsible
    D. the responsibility of the supervisor to see that clients receive adequate service

15.____

16. With respect to supervision of Worker IV, the supervisor should
    A. show the worker that resources figures are incomplete but that even if they were complete, the family would probably be eligible for assistance
    B. ask the worker why he is so protective of these families since there are three cases so similar

16.____

C. discuss with the worker all three cases at the same time so that the worker may see his own role in the three situations
D. discuss with the worker the reasons for departmental policies and procedures around budgeting

17. With respect to supervision of Workers I and IV, since these two workers are friends and would seem to be influencing each other, the supervisor should 17.____
    A. hold a joint conference with them both, pointing out how they should clear with the supervisor and not make their own rules together
    B. handle the problems of each separately in individual conferences
    C. separate them by transferring one to another territory or another unit
    D. take up the problem of workers asking help of each other rather than from the supervisor in a group meeting

Questions 18-20.

DIRECTIONS: Questions 18 through 20 are to be answered SOLELY on the basis of the following passage.

One of the key supervisory problems in a large municipal recreation department is that many leaders are assigned to isolated playgrounds or small centers, where it is difficult to observe their work regularly. Often their facilities are extremely limited. In such settings, as well as in larger recreation centers, where many recreation leaders tend to have other jobs as well, there tends to be a low level of morale and incentive. Still, it is the supervisor's task to help recreation personnel to develop pride in their work and to maintain a high level of performance. With isolated leaders, the supervisor may give advice or assistance. Leaders may be assigned to different tasks or settings during the year to maximize their productivity and provide new challenges. When it is clear that leaders are no willing to make a real effort to contribute to the department, the possibility of penalties must be considered, within the scope of departmental policy and the union contract. However, the supervisor should be constructive, encourage and assist workers to take a greater interest in their work, be innovative, and try to raise morale and to improve performance in positive ways.

18. The one of the following that would the MOST appropriate title for the above passage is 18.____
    A. Small Community Centers – Pro and Con
    B. Planning Better Recreation Programs
    C. The Supervisor's Task in Upgrading Personnel Performance
    D. The Supervisor and the Municipal Union – Rights and Obligations

19. The above passage makes clear that recreation leadership performance in all recreation playgrounds and centers throughout a large city is 19.____
    A. generally above average, with good morale on the part of most recreation leaders
    B. beyond description since no one has ever observed or evaluated recreation leaders

C. a key test of the personnel department's effort to develop more effective hiring standards
D. of mixed quality, with many recreation leaders having poor morale and a low level of achievement

20. According to the above passage, the supervisor's role is to  20._____
    A. use disciplinary action as his major tool in upgrading performance
    B. tolerate the lack of effort of individual employees since they are assigned to isolated playgrounds or small centers
    C. employ encouragement, advice, and, when appropriate, disciplinary action to improve performance
    D. inform the county supervisor whenever malfeasance or idleness is detected

Questions 21-25.

DIRECTIONS: Questions 21 through 25 are to be answered SOLELY on the basis of the following passage.

## EMPLOYEE LEAVE REGULATIONS

Peter Smith, as a full-time permanent city employee under the Career and Salary Plan, earns an *annual leave allowance*. This consists of a certain number of days off a year with pay and may be used for vacation, personal business, and for observing religious holidays. As a newly appointed employee, during his first 8 years of city service, he will earn an annual leave allowance of 20 days off a year (an average of $1^2/_3$ days off a month). After he has finished 8 full years of working for the city, he will begin earning an additional 5 days off a year. His annual leave allowance, therefore, will then be 25 days a year and will remain at this amount for seven full years. He will begin earning an additional two days off a year at this amount for seven full years. He will begin earning an additional two days off a year after he has completed a total of 15 years of city employment. Therefore, in his sixteenth year of working for the city, Mr. Smith will be earning 27 days off a year as his annual leave allowance (an average of $2¼$ days off a month).

A *sick leave allowance* of one day a month is also given to Mr. Smith, but it can be used only in cases of actual illness. When Mr. Smith returns to work after using sick leave allowance, he must have a doctor's note if the absence is for a total of more than 3 days, but he may also be required to show a doctor's note for absences of 1, 2, or 3 days.

21. According to the above passage, Mr. Smith's annual leave allowance consists  21._____
    of a certain number of days off a year which he
    A. does not get paid for
    B. gets paid for at time and a half
    C. may use for personal business
    D. may not use for observing religious holidays

22. According to the above passage, after Mr. Smith has been working for the city  22._____
    for 9 years, his annual leave allowance will be _____ days a year.
    A. 20        B. 25        C. 27        D. 37

23. According to the above passage, Mr. Smith will begin earning an average of 2 days off a month as his annual leave allowance after he has worked for the city for _____ full years.
    A. 7   B. 8   C. 15   D. 17

24. According to the above passage, Mr. Smith is given a sick leave allowance of
    A. 1 day every 2 months
    B. 1 day per month
    C. 1⅔ days per month
    D. 2¼ days a month

25. According to the above passage, when he uses sick leave allowance, Mr. Smith may be required to show a doctor's note
    A. even if his absence is for only 1 day
    B. only if his absence is for more than 2 days
    C. only if his absence is for more than 3 days
    D. only if his absence is for 3 days or more

# KEY (CORRECT ANSWERS)

| | | | |
|---|---|---|---|
| 1. | C | 11. | A |
| 2. | C | 12. | D |
| 3. | D | 13. | D |
| 4. | A | 14. | A |
| 5. | B | 15. | C |
| 6. | B | 16. | C |
| 7. | A | 17. | B |
| 8. | D | 18. | C |
| 9. | B | 19. | D |
| 10. | C | 20. | C |

21. C
22. B
23. C
24. B
25. A

# TEST 3

DIRECTIONS: Each question or incomplete statement is followed by several suggested answers or completions. Select the one that BEST answers the question or completes the statement. *PRINT THE LETTER OF THE CORRECT ANSWER IN THE SPACE AT THE RIGHT.*

Questions 1-6.

DIRECTIONS: Questions 1 through 6 are to be answered SOLELY on the basis of the following passage.

    A folder is made of a sheet of heavy paper (manila, kraft, pressboard, or red rope stock) that has been folded once so that the back is about one-half inch higher than the front. Folders are larger than the papers they contain in order to protect them. Two standard folder sizes are *letter size* for papers that are 8½" x 11" and *legal cap* for papers that are 8½" x 13".
    Folders are cut across the top in two ways: so that the back is straight (straight-cut) or so that the back has a tab that projects above the top of the folder. Such tabs bear captions that identify the contents of each folder. Tabs vary in width and position. The tabs of a set of folders that are *one-half cut* are half the width of the folder and have only two positions.
    *One-third cut* folders have three positions, each tab occupying a third of the width of the folder. Another standard tabbing is *one-fifth cut*, which has five positions. There are also folders with *two-fifths cut*, with the tabs in the third and fourth or fourth and fifth positions.

1. Of the following, the BEST title for the above passage is
   A. Filing Folders
   B. Standard Folder Sizes
   C. The Uses of the Folder
   D. The Use of Tabs

2. According to the above passage, one of the standard folder sizes is called
   A. Kraft cut
   B. legal cap
   C. one-half cut
   D. straight-cut

3. According to the above passage, tabs are GENERALLY placed along the _____ of the folder.
   A. back    B. front    C. left side    D. right side

4. According to the above passage, a tab is GENERALLY used to
   A. distinguish between standard folder sizes
   B. identify the contents of a folder
   C. increase the size of the folder
   D. protect the papers within the folder

5. According to the above passage, a folder that is two-fifths cut has _____ tabs.
   A. no    B. two    C. three    D. five

6. According to the above passage, one reason for making folders larger than the papers they contain is that
   A. only a certain size folder can be made from heavy paper
   B. they will protect the papers
   C. they will aid in setting up a tab system
   D. the back of the folder must be higher than the front

6.____

Questions 7-15.

DIRECTIONS: Questions 7 through 15 are to be answered SOLELY on the basis of the following passage.

The City University of New York traces its origins to 1847, when the Free Academy, which later became City College, was founded as the first tuition-free municipal college. City and Hunter Colleges were placed under the direction of the Board of Higher Education in 1926, and Brooklyn and Queens Colleges were subsequently added to the system of municipal colleges. In 1955, Staten Island Community College, the first of the two-year colleges sponsored by the Board of Higher Education under the program of the State University of New York, joined the system.

In 1961, the four senior colleges and three community colleges then under the jurisdiction of the Board of Higher Education became the City University of New York, and a University Graduate Division was organized to offer programs leading to the Ph.D. Since then, the university has undergone even more rapid growth. Today, it consists of nine senior colleges, an upper division college which admits students at the junior level, eight community colleges, a graduate division, and an affiliated medical center.

In the summer of 1969, the Board of Higher Education resolved that the time had come to commit the resources of the university to meeting an urgent social need—unrestricted access to higher education for all youths of the City. Determined to prevent the waste of human potential represented by the thousands of high school graduates whose limited educational opportunities left them unable to meet existing admission standards, the Board moved to adopt a policy of Open Admissions. It was their judgment that the best way of determining whether a potential student can benefit from college work is to admit him to college, provide him with the learning assistance he needs, and then evaluate his performance.

Beginning with the class of June 1970, every New York City resident who received a high school diploma from a public or private high school was guaranteed a place in one of the colleges of City University.

7. Of the following, the BEST title for the above passage is
   A. A Brief History of the City University
   B. High Schools and the City University
   C. The Components of the University
   D. Tuition-free Colleges

7.____

8. According to the above passage, which one of the following colleges of the City University was ORIGINALLY called the Free Academy?
   A. Brooklyn College     B. City College
   C. Hunter College       D. Queens College

8.____

9. According to the above passage, the system of municipal colleges became the  9.____
City University of New York in
   A. 1926   B. 1955   C. 1961   D. 1969

10. According to the above passage, Staten Island Community College came  10.____
under the jurisdiction of the Board of Higher Education
   A. 6 years after a Graduate Division was organized
   B. 8 years before the adoption of the Open Admissions Policy
   C. 29 years after Brooklyn and Queens Colleges
   D. 29 years after City and Hunter Colleges

11. According to the above passage, the Staten Island Community College is  11.____
   A. a graduate division center   B. a senior college
   C. a two-year college   D. an upper division college

12. According to the above passage, the TOTAL number of colleges, divisions,  12.____
and affiliated branches of the City University is
   A. 18   B. 19   C. 20   D. 21

13. According to the above passage, the Open Admissions Policy is designed  13.____
to determine whether a potential student will benefit from college by
PRIMARILY
   A. discouraging competition for placement in the City University among high school students
   B. evaluating his performance after entry into college
   C. lowering admission standards
   D. providing learning assistance before entry into college

14. According to the above passage, the FIRST class to be affected by the Open  14.____
Admissions Policy was the
   A. high school class which graduated in January 1970
   B. City University class which graduated in June 1970
   C. high school class when graduated in June 1970
   D. City University class when graduated in June 1970

15. According to the above passage, one of the reasons that the Board of Higher  15.____
Education initiated the policy of Open Admission was to
   A. enable high school graduates with a background of limited educational opportunities to enter college
   B. expand the growth of the City University so as to increase the number and variety of degrees offered
   C. provide a social resource to the qualified youth of the City
   D. revise admission standards to meet the needs of the City

4 (#3)

Questions 16-18.

DIRECTIONS:  Questions 16 through 18 are to be answered SOLELY on the basis of the following passage.

Hereafter, all probationary students interested in transferring to community college career programs (associate degrees) from liberal arts programs in senior colleges (bachelor degrees) will be eligible for such transfers if they have completed no more than three semesters.
For students with averages 1.5 or above, transfer will be automatic. Those with 1.0 to 1.5 averages can transfer provisionally and will be required to make substantial progress during the first semester in the career program. Once transfer has taken place, only those courses in which passing grades were received will be computed in the community college grade-point average.
No request for transfer will be accepted from probationary students wishing to enter the liberal arts programs at the community college.

16. According to the above passage, the one of the following which is the BEST statement concerning the transfer of probationary students is that a probationary student
    A. may transfer to a career program at the end of one semester
    B. must complete three semester hours before he is eligible for transfer
    C. is not eligible to transfer to a career program
    D. is eligible to transfer to a liberal arts program

16.____

17. Which of the following is the BEST statement of academic evaluation for transfer purposes in the case of probationary students?
    A. No probationary student with an average under 1.5 may transfer.
    B. A probationary student with an average of 1.3 may not transfer.
    C. A probationary student with an average of 1.6 may transfer.
    D. A probationary student with an average of .8 may transfer on a provisional basis.

17.____

18. It is MOST likely that, of the following, the next degree sought by one who already holds the Associate in Science degree would be a(n) _____ degree.
    A. Assistantship in Science      B. Associate in Applied Science
    C. Bachelor of Science           D. Doctor of Philosophy

18.____

Questions 19-20.

DIRECTIONS:  Questions 19 and 20 are to be answered SOLELY on the basis of the following passage.

Auto: Auto travel requires prior approval by the President and/or appropriate Dean and must be indicated in the *Request for Travel Authorization* form. Employees authorized to use personal autos on official College business will be reimbursed at the rate of 28¢ per mile for the first 500 miles driven and 18¢ per mile for mileage driven in excess of 500 mile. The Comptroller's Office may limit the amount of reimbursement to the expenditure that would have been made if a less expensive mode of transportation (railroad, airplane, bus, etc.) had been utilized. If this occurs, the traveler will have to pick up the excess expenditure as a personal expense.

Tolls, Parking Fees, and Parking Meter Fees are not reimbursable and many not be claimed.

19. Suppose that Professor T gives the office assistant the following memorandum: Used car for official trip to Albany, New York, and return. Distance from New York to Albany is 148 miles. Tolls were $3.50 each way. Parking garage cost $3.00. When preparing the Travel Expense Voucher for Professor T, the figure which should be claimed for transportation is
    A. $120.88    B. $113.88    C. $82.88    D. $51.44

    19.____

20. Suppose that Professor V gives the office assistant the following memorandum: Used car for official trip to Pittsburgh, Pennsylvania, and return. Distance from New York to Pittsburgh is 350 miles. Tolls were $3.30, $11.40 going, and $3.30, $2.00 returning.
    When preparing the Travel Expense Voucher for Professor V, the figure which should be claimed for transportation is
    A. $225.40    B. $176.00    C. $127.40    D. $98.00

    20.____

Questions 21-25.

DIRECTIONS:   Questions 21 through 25 are to be answered SOLELY on the basis of the following passage.

For a period of nearly fifteen years, beginning in the mid-1950's, higher education sustained a phenomenal rate of growth. The factor principally responsible were continuing improvement in the rate of college entrance by high school graduates, a 50 percent increase in the size of the college-age (eighteen to twenty-one) group and—until about 1967—a rapid expansion of university research activity supported by the Federal government.

Today, as one looks ahead to the year 2010, it is apparent that each of these favorable stimuli will either be abated or turn into a negative factor. The rate of growth of the college-age group has already diminished; and from 2000 to 2005, the size of the college-age group has shrunk annually almost as fast as it grew from 1965 to 1970. From 2005 to 2010, this annual decrease will slow down so that by 2010 the age group will be about the same size as it was in 2009. This substantial net decrease in the size of the college-age group (from 1995 to 2010) will dramatically affect college enrollments since, currently, 83 percent of undergraduates are twenty-one and under, and another 11 percent are twenty-to to twenty-four.

21. Which one of the following factors is NOT mentioned in the above passage as contributing to the high rate of growth of higher education?
    A. A large increase in the size of the eighteen to twenty-one age group
    B. The equalization of educational opportunities among socio-economic groups
    C. The Federal budget impact on research and development spending in the higher education sector
    D. The increasing rate at which high school graduates enter college

    21.____

22. Based on the information in the above passage, the size of the college-age group in 2010 will be
    A. larger than it was in 2009
    B. larger than it was in 1995
    C. smaller than it was in 2005
    D. about the same as it was in 2000

23. According to the above passage, the tremendous rate of growth of higher education started around
    A. 1950   B. 1955   C. 1960   D. 1965

24. The percentage of undergraduates who are over age 24 is MOST NEARLY
    A. 6%   B. 8%   C. 11%   D. 17%

25. Which one of the following conclusions can be substantiated by the information given in the above passage?
    A. The college-age group was about the same size in 2000 as it was in 1965.
    B. The annual decrease in the size of the college-age group from 2000 to 2005 is about the same as the annual increase from 1965 to 1970.
    C. The overall decrease in the size of the college-age group from 2000 to 2005 will be followed by an overall increase in its size from 2005 to 2010.
    D. The size of the college-age group is decreasing at a fairly constant rate from 1995 to 2010.

# KEY (CORRECT ANSWERS)

| | | | |
|---|---|---|---|
| 1. | A | 11. | C |
| 2. | B | 12. | C |
| 3. | A | 13. | B |
| 4. | B | 14. | C |
| 5. | B | 15. | A |
| 6. | B | 16. | A |
| 7. | A | 17. | C |
| 8. | B | 18. | C |
| 9. | C | 19. | C |
| 10. | D | 20. | B |

| | |
|---|---|
| 21. | B |
| 22. | C |
| 23. | B |
| 24. | A |
| 25. | B |

# REPORT WRITING
# EXAMINATION SECTION
## TEST 1

DIRECTIONS: Each question or incomplete statement is followed by several suggested answers or completions. Select the one that BEST answers the question or completes the statement. *PRINT THE LETTER OF THE CORRECT ANSWER IN THE SPACE AT THE RIGHT.*

Questions 1-4.

DIRECTIONS: Answer Questions 1 through 4 on the basis of the following report which was prepared by a supervisor for inclusion in his agency's annual report.

Line #
1  On Oct. 13, I was assigned to study the salaries paid.
2  to clerical employees in various titles by the city and by
3  private industry in the area.
4  In order to get the data I needed, I called Mr. Johnson at
5  the Bureau of the Budget and the payroll officers at X Corp.—
6  a brokerage house, Y Co. —an insurance company, and Z Inc. —
7  a publishing firm. None of them was available and I had to call
8  all of them again the next day.
9  When I finally got the information I needed, I drew up a
10 chart, which is attached. Note that not all of the companies I
11 contacted employed people at all the different levels used in the
12 city service.
13 The conclusions I draw from analyzing this information is
14 as follows: The city's entry-level salary is about average for
15 the region; middle-level salaries are generally higher in the
16 city government plan than in private industry; but salaries at the
17 highest levels in private industry are better than city em-
18 ployees' pay.

1. Which of the following criticisms about the style in which this report is written is MOST valid?　　　　　　　　　　　　　　　　　　　　　　　　1.____
   A. It is too informal.　　　　　　　B. It is too concise.
   C. It is too choppy.　　　　　　　　D. The syntax is too complex.

2. Judging from the statements made in the report, the method followed by this employee in performing his research was　　　　　　　　　　　　　　　　2.____
   A. *good*; he contacted a representative sample of businesses in the area
   B. *poor*; he should have drawn more definite conclusions
   C. *good*; he was persistent in collecting information
   D. *poor*; he did not make a thorough study

3. One sentence in this report contains a grammatical error. This sentence begins on line number
   A. 4   B. 7   C. 10   D. 14

4. The type of information given in this report which should be presented in footnotes or in an appendix is the
   A. purpose of the study
   B. specifics about the businesses contacted
   C. reference to the chart
   D. conclusions drawn by the author

5. The use of a graph to show statistical data in a report is SUPERIOR to a table because it
   A. features approximations
   B. emphasizes facts and relationships more dramatically
   C. presents data more accurately
   D. is easily understood by the average reader

6. Of the following, the degree of formality required of a written report in tone is MOST likely to depend on the
   A. subject matter of the report
   B. frequency of its occurrence
   C. amount of time available for its preparation
   D. audience for whom the report is intended

7. Of the following, a distinguishing characteristic of a written report intended for the head of your agency as compared to a report prepared for a lower-echelon staff member is that the report for the agency head should USUALLY include
   A. considerably more detail, especially statistical data
   B. the essential details in an abbreviated form
   C. all available source material
   D. an annotated bibliography

8. Assume that you are asked to write a lengthy report for use by the administrator of your agency, the subject of which is "The Impact of Proposed New Data Processing Operation on Line Personnel" in your agency. You decide that the *most* appropriate type of report for you to prepare is an analytical report, including recommendations.
   The MAIN reason for your decision is that
   A. the subject of the report is extremely complex
   B. large sums of money are involved
   C. the report is being prepared for the administrator
   D. you intend to include charts and graphs

9. Assume that you are preparing a report based on a survey dealing with the attitudes of employees in Division X regarding proposed new changes in compensating employees for working overtime. Three percent of the respondents to the survey voluntarily offer an unfavorable opinion on the method of assigning overtime work, a question not specifically asked of the employees.
On the basis of this information, the MOST appropriate and significant of the following comments for you to make in the report with regard to employees' attitudes on assigning overtime work is that
   A. an insignificant percentage of employees dislike the method of assigning overtime work
   B. three percent of the employees in Division X dislike the method of assigning overtime work
   C. three percent of the sample selected for the survey voiced an unfavorable opinion on the method of assigning overtime work
   D. some employees voluntarily voiced negative feelings about the method of assigning overtime work, making it impossible to determine the extent of this attitude

10. A supervisor should be able to prepare a report that is well-written and unambiguous.
Of the following sentences that might appear in a report, select the one which communicates MOST clearly the intent of its author.
   A. When your subordinates speak to a group of people, they should be well-informed.
   B. When he asked him to leave, SanMan King told him that he would refuse the request.
   C. Because he is a good worker, Foreman Jefferson assigned Assistant Foreman D'Agostino to replace him.
   D. Each of us is responsible for the actions of our subordinates.

11. In some reports, especially longer ones, a list of the resources (books, papers, magazines, etc.) used to prepare it is included. This list is called the
   A. accreditation          B. bibliography
   C. summary                D. glossary

12. Reports are usually divided into several sections, some of which are more necessary than others.
Of the following, the section which is ABSOLUTELY necessary to include in a report is
   A. a table of contents    B. the body
   C. an index               D. a bibliography

13. Suppose you are writing a report on an interview you have just completed with a particularly hostile applicant.
    Which of the following BEST describes what you should include in this report?
    A. What you think caused the applicant's hostile attitude during the interview
    B. Specific examples of the applicant's hostile remarks and behavior
    C. The relevant information uncovered during the interview
    D. A recommendation that the applicant's request be denied because of his hostility

14. When including recommendations in a report to your supervisor, which of the following is MOST important for you to do?
    A. Provide several alternative courses of action for each recommendation
    B. First present the supporting evidence, then the recommendations
    C. First present the recommendations, then the supporting evidence
    D. Make sure the recommendations arise logically out of the information in the report

15. It is often necessary that the writer of a report present facts and sufficient arguments to gain acceptance of the points, conclusions, or recommendations set forth in the report.
    Of the following, the LEAST advisable step to take in organizing a report, when such argumentation is the important factor, is a(n)
    A. elaborate expression of personal belief
    B. businesslike discussion of the problem as a whole
    C. orderly arrangement of convincing data
    D. reasonable explanation of the primary issues

16. In some types of reports, visual aids add interest, meaning, and support. They also provide an essential means of effectively communicating the message of the report.
    Of the following, the selection of the suitable visual aids to use with a report is LEAST dependent on the
    A. nature and scope of the report
    B. way in which the aid is to be used
    C. aid used in other reports
    D. prospective readers of the report

17. Visual aids used in a report may be placed either in the text material or in the appendix.
    Deciding where to put a chart, table, or any such aid should depend on the
    A. title of the report           B. purpose of the visual aid
    C. title of the visual aid       D. length of the report

18. A report is often revised several times before final preparation and distribution in an effort to make certain the report meets the needs of the situation for which it is designed.
    Which of the following is the BEST way for the author to be sure that a report covers the areas he intended?

A. Obtain a coworker's opinion
B. Compare it with a content checklist
C. Test it on a subordinate
D. Check his bibliography

19. In which of the following situations is an oral report preferable to a written report?  When a(n)
    A. recommendation is being made for a future plan of action
    B. department head requests immediate information
    C. long-standing policy change is made
    D. analysis of complicated statistical data is involved

    19.____

20. When an applicant is approved, the supervisor must fill in standard forms with certain information.
    The GREATEST advantage of using standard forms in this situation rather than having the supervisor write the report as he sees fit is that
    A. the report can be acted on quickly
    B. the report can be written without directions from a supervisor
    C. needed information is less likely to be left out of the report
    D. information that is written up this way is more likely to be verified

    20.____

21. Assume that it is part of your job to prepare a monthly report for your unit head that eventually goes to the director.  The report contains information on the number of applicants you have interviewed that have been approved and the number of applicants you have interviewed that have been turned down.
    Errors on such reports are serious because
    A. you are expected to be able to prove how many applicants you have interviewed each month
    B. accurate statistics are needed for effective management of the department
    C. they may not be discovered before the report is transmitted to the director
    D. they may result in loss to the applicants left out of the report

    21.____

22. The frequency with which job reports are submitted should depend MAINLY on
    A. how comprehensive the report has to be
    B. the amount of information in the report
    C. the availability of an experienced man to write the report
    D. the importance of changes in the information included in the report

    22.____

23. The CHIEF purpose in preparing an outline for a report is usually to insure that
    A. the report will be grammatically correct
    B. every point will be given equal emphasis
    C. principal and secondary points will be properly integrated
    D. the language of the report will be of the same level and include the same technical terms

    23.____

24. The MAIN reason for requiring written job reports is to  24.____
    A. avoid the necessity of oral orders
    B. develop better methods of doing the work
    C. provide a permanent record of what was done
    D. increase the amount of work that can be done

25. Assume you are recommending in a report to your supervisor that a radical  25.____
    change in a standard maintenance procedure should be adopted.
    Of the following, the MOST important information to be included in this report is
    A. a list of the reasons for making this change
    B. the names of others who favor the change
    C. a complete description of the present procedure
    D. amount of training time needed for the new procedure

## KEY (CORRECT ANSWERS)

| | | | |
|---|---|---|---|
| 1. | A | 11. | B |
| 2. | D | 12. | B |
| 3. | D | 13. | C |
| 4. | B | 14. | D |
| 5. | B | 15. | A |
| 6. | D | 16. | C |
| 7. | B | 17. | B |
| 8. | A | 18. | B |
| 9. | D | 19. | B |
| 10. | D | 20. | C |

| | |
|---|---|
| 21. | B |
| 22. | D |
| 23. | C |
| 24. | C |
| 25. | A |

# TEST 2

DIRECTIONS: Each question or incomplete statement is followed by several suggested answers or completions. Select the one that BEST answers the question or completes the statement. *PRINT THE LETTER OF THE CORRECT ANSWER IN THE SPACE AT THE RIGHT.*

1. It is often necessary that the writer of a report present facts and sufficient arguments to gain acceptance of the points, conclusions, or recommendations set forth in the report.
   Of the following, the LEAST advisable step to take in organizing a report, when such argumentation is the important factor, is a(n)
   A. elaborate expression of personal belief
   B. businesslike discussion of the problem as a whole
   C. orderly arrangement of convincing data
   D. reasonable explanation of the primary issues

   1._____

2. Of the following, the factor which is generally considered to be LEAST characteristic of a good control report is that it
   A. stresses performance that adheres to standard rather than emphasizing the exception
   B. supplies information intended to serve as the basis for corrective action
   C. provides feedback for the planning process
   D. includes data that reflect trends as well as current status

   2._____

3. An administrative assistant has been asked by his superior to write a concise, factual report with objective conclusions and recommendations based on facts assembled by other researchers.
   Of the following factors, the administrative assistant should give LEAST consideration to
   A. the educational level of the person or persons for whom the report is being prepared
   B. the use to be made of the report
   C. the complexity of the problem
   D. his own feelings about the importance of the problem

   3._____

4. When making a written report, it is often recommended that the findings or conclusions be presented near the beginning of the report.
   Of the following, the MOST important reason for doing this is that it
   A. facilitates organizing the material clearly
   B. assures that all the topics will be covered
   C. avoids unnecessary repetition of ideas
   D. prepares the reader for the facts that will follow

   4._____

5. You have been asked to write a report on methods of hiring and training new employees. Your report is going to be about ten pages long.
For the convenience of your readers, a brief summary of your findings should
   A. appear at the beginning of your report
   B. be appended to the report as a postscript
   C. be circulated in a separate memo
   D. be inserted in tabular form in the middle of your report

6. In preparing a report, the MAIN reason for writing an outline is usually to
   A. help organize thoughts in a logical sequence
   B. provide a guide for the typing of the report
   C. allow the ultimate user to review the report in advance
   D. ensure that the report is being prepared on schedule

7. The one of the following which is MOST appropriate as a reason for including footnotes in a report is to
   A. correct capitalization
   B. delete passages
   C. improve punctuation
   D. cite references

8. A completed formal report may contain all of the following EXCEPT
   A. a synopsis
   B. a preface
   C. marginal notes
   D. bibliographical references

9. Of the following, the MAIN use of proofreaders' marks is to
   A. explain corrections to be made
   B. indicate that a manuscript has been read and approved
   C. let the reader know who proofread the report
   D. indicate the format of the report

10. Informative, readable, and concise reports have been found to observe the following rules:
    Rule I. Keep the report short and easy to understand
    Rule II. Vary the length of sentences.
    Rule III. Vary the style of sentences so that, for example, they are not all just subject-verb, subject-verb.
    Consider this hospital laboratory report: The experiment was started in January. The apparatus was put together in six weeks. At that time, the synthesizing process was begun. The synthetic chemicals were separated. Then they were used in tests on patients.
    Which one of the following choices MOST accurately classifies the above rules into those which are violated by this report ad those which are not?
    A. II is violated, but I and III are not.
    B. III is violated, but I and II are not.
    C. II and III are violated, but I is not.
    D. I, II, and III are violated,

Questions 11-13.

DIRECTIONS: Questions 11 through 13 are based on the following example of a report. The report consists of eight numbered sentences, some of which are not consistent with the principles of good report writing.

(1) I interviewed Mrs. Loretta Crawford in Room 424 of County Hospital. (2) She had collapsed on the street and been brought into emergency. (3) She is an attractive woman with many friends judging by the cards she had received. (4) She did not know what her husband's last job had been, or what their present income was. (5) The first thing that Mrs. Crawford said was that she had never worked and that her husband was presently unemployed. (6) She did not know if they had any medical coverage or if they could pay the bill. (7) She said that her husband could not be reached by telephone but that he would be in to see her that afternoon. (8) I left word at the nursing station to be called when he arrived.

11. A good report should be arranged in logical order.
    Which of the following sentences from the report does NOT appear in its proper sequence in the report?
    A. 1   B. 4   C. 7   D. 8

12. Only material that is relevant to the main thought of a report should be included.
    Which of the following sentences from the report contains material which is LEAST relevant to this report?  Sentence
    A. 3   B. 4   C. 6   D. 8

13. Reports should include all essential information.
    Of the following, the MOST important fact that is missing from this report is:
    A. Who was involved in the interview
    B. What was discovered at the interview
    C. When the interview took place
    D. Where the interview took place

Questions 14-15.

DIRECTIONS: Each of Questions 14 and 15 consists of four numbered sentences which constitute a paragraph in a report. They are not in the right order. Choose the numbered arrangement appearing after letter A, B, C, or D which is MOST logical and which BEST expresses the thought of the paragraph.

14. I.  Congress made the commitment explicit in the Housing Act of 1949, establishing as a national goal the realization of a decent home and suitable environment for every American family.
    II. The result has been that the goal of decent home and suitable environment is still as far distant as ever for the disadvantaged urban family
    III. In spite of this action by Congress, federal housing programs have continued to be fragmented and grossly under-funded.
    IV. The passage of the National Housing Act signaled a new federal commitment to provide housing for the nation's citizens.

The CORRECT answer is:
A. I, IV, III, II  B. IV, I, III, II  C. IV, I, III, II  D. II, IV, I, III

15. 
I. The greater expense does not necessarily involve "exploitation," but it is often perceived as exploitative and unfair by those who are aware of the price differences involved, but unaware of operating costs.
II. Ghetto residents believe they are "exploited" by local merchants, and evidence substantiates some of these beliefs.
III. However, stores in low-income areas were more likely to be small independents, which could not achieve the economies available to supermarket chains and were, therefore, more likely to charge higher prices, and the customers were more likely to buy smaller-sized packages which are more expensive per unit of measure.
IV. A study conducted in one city showed that distinctly higher prices were charged for goods sold in ghetto stores than in other areas.

The CORRECT answer is:
A. IV, II, I, III  B. IV, I, III, II  C. II, IV, III, I  D. II, III, IV, I

16. In organizing data to be presented in a formal report, the FIRST of the following steps should be
    A. determining the conclusions to be drawn
    B. establishing the time sequence of the data
    C. sorting and arranging like data into groups
    D. evaluating how consistently the data support the recommendations

17. All reports should be prepared with at least one copy so that
    A. there is one copy for your file
    B. there is a copy for your supervisor
    C. the report can be sent to more than one person
    D. the person getting the report can forward a copy to someone else

18. Before turning in a report of an investigation he has made, a supervisor discovers some additional information he did not include in this report. Whether he rewrites this report to include this additional information should PRIMARILY depend on the
    A. importance of the report itself
    B. number of people who will eventually review this report
    C. established policy covering the subject matter of the report
    D. bearing this new information has on the conclusions of the report

## KEY (CORRECT ANSWERS)

1. A
2. A
3. D
4. D
5. A

6. A
7. D
8. C
9. A
10. C

11. B
12. A
13. C
14. B
15. C

16. C
17. A
18. D

# EXAMINATION SECTION
## TEST 1

DIRECTIONS: In each of the following questions, only one of the four sentences conforms to standards of correct usage. The other three contain errors in grammar, diction, or punctuation. Select the choice in each question which BEST conforms to standards of correct usage. Consider a choice correct if it contains none of the errors mentioned above, even though there may be other ways of expressing the same thought. *PRINT THE LETTER OF THE CORRECT ANSWER IN THE SPACE AT THE RIGHT.*

1. 
   A. Because he was ill was no excuse for his behavior
   B. I insist that he see a lawyer before he goes to trial.
   C. He said "that he had not intended to go."
   D. He wasn't out of the office only three days.

   1.____

2. 
   A. He came to the station and pays a porter to carry his bags into the train.
   B. I should have liked to live in medieval times.
   C. My father was born in Linville. A little country town where everybody knows everyone else.
   D. The car, which is parked across the street, is disabled.

   2.____

3. 
   A. He asked the desk clerk for a clean, quiet, room.
   B. I expected James to be lonesome and that he would want to go home.
   C. I have stopped worrying because I have heard nothing further on the subject.
   D. If the board of directors controls the company, they may take actions which are disapproved by the stockholders.

   3.____

4. 
   A. Each of the players knew their place.
   B. He whom you saw on the stage is the son of an actor.
   C. Susan is the smartest of the twin sisters.
   D. Who ever thought of him winning both prizes?

   4.____

5. 
   A. An outstanding trait of early man was their reliance on omens.
   B. Because I had never been there before.
   C. Neither Mr. Jones nor Mr. Smith has completed his work.
   D. While eating my dinner, a dog came to the window.

   5.____

6. 
   A. A copy of the lease, in addition to the Rules and Regulations, are to be given to each tenant.
   B. The Rules and Regulations and a copy of the lease is being given to each tenant.
   C. A copy of the lease, in addition to the Rules and Regulations, is to be given to each tenant.
   D. A copy of the lease, in addition to the Rules and Regulations, are being given to each tenant.

   6.____

7.  A. Although we understood that for him music was a passion, we were disturbed by the fact that he was addicted to sing along with the soloists.
    B. Do you believe that Steven is liable to win a scholarship?
    C. Give the picture to whomever is a connoisseur of art.
    D. Whom do you believe to be the most efficient worker in the office?

8.  A. Each adult who is sure they know all the answers will some day realize their mistake.
    B. Even the most hardhearted villain would have to feel bad about so horrible a tragedy.
    C. Neither being licensed teachers, both aspirants had to pass rigorous tests before being appointed.
    D. The principal reason why he wanted to be designated was because he had never before been to a convention.

9.  A. Being that the weather was so inclement, the party has been postponed for at least a month.
    B. He is in New York City only three weeks and he has already seen all the thrilling sights in Manhattan and in the other four boroughs.
    C. If you will look it up in the official directory, which can be consulted in the library during specified hours, you will discover that the chairman and director are Mr. T. Henry Long.
    D. Working hard at college during the day and at the post office during the night, he appeared to his family to be indefatigable.

10. A. I would have been happy to oblige you if you only asked me to do it.
    B. The cold weather, as well as the unceasing wind and rain, have made us decide to spend the winter in Florida.
    C. The politician would have been more successful in winning office if he would have been less dogmatic.
    D. These trousers are expensive; however, they will wear well.

11. A. All except him wore formal attire at the reception for the ambassador.
    B. If that chair were to be blown off of the balcony, it might injure someone below.
    C. Not a passenger, who was in the crash, survived the impact.
    D. To borrow money off friends is the best way to lose them.

12. A. Approaching Manhattan on the ferry boat from Staten Island, an unforgettable sight of the skyscrapers is seen.
    B. Did you see the exhibit of modernistic paintings as yet?
    C. Gesticulating wildly and ranting in stentorian tones, the speaker was the sinecure of all eyes.
    D. The airplane with crew and passengers was lost somewhere in the Pacific Ocean.

13. A. If one has consistently had that kind of training, it is certainly too late to change your entire method of swimming long distances.
    B. The captain would have been more impressed if you would have been more conscientious in evacuation drills.
    C. The passengers on the stricken ship were all ready to abandon it at the signal.
    D. The villainous shark lashed at the lifeboat with it's tail, trying to upset the rocking boat in order to partake of it's contents.

13.____

14. A. As one whose been certified as a professional engineer, I believe that the decision to build a bridge over that harbor is unsound.
    B. Between you and me, this project ought to be completed long before winter arrives.
    C. He fervently hoped that the men would be back at camp and to find them busy at their usual chores.
    D. Much to his surprise, he discovered that the climate of Korea was like his home town.

14.____

15. A. An industrious executive is aided, not impeded, by having a hobby which gives him a fresh point of view on life and its problems.
    B. Frequent absence during the calendar year will surely mitigate against the chances of promotion.
    C. He was unable to go to the committee meeting because he was very ill.
    D. Mr. Brown expressed his disapproval so emphatically that his associates were embarassed

15.____

16. A. At our next session, the office manager will have told you something about his duties and responsibilities.
    B. In general, the book is absorbing and original and have no hesitation about recommending it.
    C. The procedures followed by private industry in dealing with lateness and absence are different from ours.
    D We shall treat confidentially any information about Mr. Doe, to whom we understand you have sent reports to for many years.

16.____

17. A. I talked to one official, whom I knew was fully impartial.
    B. Everyone signed the petition but him.
    C. He proved not only to be a good student but also a good athlete.
    D. All are incorrect.

17.____

18. A. Every year a large amount of tenants are admitted to housing projects.
    B. Henry Ford owned around a billion dollars in industrial equipment.
    C. He was aggravated by the child's poor behavior.
    D. All are incorrect.

18.____

19. A. Before he was committed to the asylum he suffered from the illusion that he was Napoleon.  19.____
    B. Besides stocks, there were also bonds in the safe.
    C. We bet the other team easily.
    D. All are incorrect.

20. A. Bring this report to your supervisory.  20.____
    B. He set the chair down near the table.
    C. The capitol of New York is Albany.
    D. All are incorrect.

21. A. He was chosen to arbitrate the dispute because everyone knew he would be disinterested.  21.____
    B. It is advisable to obtain the best council before making an important decision.
    C. Less college students are interested in teaching than ever before.
    D. All are incorrect.

22. A. She, hearing a signal, the source lamp flashed.  22.____
    B. While hearing a signal, the source lamp flashed.
    C. In hearing a signal, the source lamp flashed.
    D. As she heard a signal, the source lamp flashed.

23. A. Every one of the time records have been initialed in the designated spaces.  23.____
    B. All of the time records has been initialed in the designated spaces.
    C. Each one of the time records was initialed in the designated spaces.
    D. The time records all been initialed in the designated spaces.

24. A. If there is no one else to answer the phone, you will have to answer it.  24.____
    B. You will have to answer it yourself if no one else answers the phone.
    C. If no one else is not around to pick up the phone, you will have to do it.
    D. You will have to answer the phone when nobodys here to do it.

25. A. Dr. Barnes not in his office. What could I do for you?  25.____
    B. Dr. Barnes is not in his office. Is there something I can do for you?
    C. Since Dr. Barnes is not in his office, might there be something I may do for you?
    D. Is there any ways I can assist you since Dr. Barnes is not in his office?

26. A. She do not understand how the new console works.  26.____
    B. The way the new console works, she doesn't understand.
    C. She doesn't understand how the new console works.
    D. The new console works, so that she doesn't understand.

27. A. Certain changes in my family income must be reported as they occur.  27.____
    B. When certain changes in family income occur, it must be reported.
    C. Certain family income change must be reported as they occur.
    D. Certain changes in family income must be reported as they have been occurring.

28.  A. Each tenant has to complete the application themselves.
     B. Each of the tenants have to complete the application by himself.
     C. Each of the tenants has to complete the application himself.
     D. Each of the tenants has to complete the application by themselves.

29.  A. Yours is the only building that the construction will effect.
     B. Your's is the only building affected by the construction.
     C. The construction will only effect your building.
     D. Yours is the only building that will be affected by the construction.

30.  A. There is four tests left.
     B. The number of tests left are four.
     C. There are four tests left.
     D. Four of the tests remains.

31.  A. Each of the applicants takes a test.
     B. Each of the applicant take a test.
     C. Each of the applicants take tests.
     D. Each of the applicants have taken tests.

32.  A. The applicant, not the examiners, are ready.
     B. The applicants, not the examiners, is ready.
     C. The applicants, not the examiner, are ready.
     D. The applicant, not the examiner, are ready

33.  A. You will not progress except you practice.
     B. You will not progress without you practicing.
     C. You will not progress unless you practice.
     D. You will not progress provided you do not practice.

34.  A. Neither the director or the employees will be at the office tomorrow.
     B. Neither the director nor the employees will be at the office tomorrow.
     C. Neither the director, or the secretary nor the other employees will be at the office tomorrow.
     D. Neither the director, the secretary or the other employees will be at the office tomorrow.

35.  A. In my absence, he and her will have to finish the assignment.
     B. In my absence he and she will have to finish the assignment.
     C. In my absence she and him, they will have to finish the assignment.
     D. In my absence he and her both will have to finish the assignment.

## KEY (CORRECT ANSWERS)

| | | | | | | | |
|---|---|---|---|---|---|---|---|
| 1. | B | 11. | A | 21. | A | 31. | A |
| 2. | B | 12. | D | 22. | D | 32. | C |
| 3. | C | 13. | C | 23. | C | 33. | C |
| 4. | B | 14. | B | 24. | A | 34. | B |
| 5. | C | 15. | A | 25. | B | 35. | B |
| 6. | C | 16. | C | 26. | C | | |
| 7. | D | 17. | B | 27. | A | | |
| 8. | B | 18. | D | 28. | C | | |
| 9. | D | 19. | B | 29. | D | | |
| 10. | D | 20. | B | 30. | C | | |

# TEST 2

DIRECTIONS: Each question or incomplete statement is followed by several suggested answers or completions. Select the one that BEST answers the question or completes the statement. *PRINT THE LETTER OF THE CORRECT ANSWER IN THE SPACE AT THE RIGHT.*

Questions 1-4.

DIRECTIONS: Questions 1 through 4 consist of three sentences each. For each question, select the sentence which contains NO error in grammar or usage.

1. A. Be sure that everybody brings his notes to the conference. 1.____
   B. He looked like he meant to hit the boy.
   C. Mr. Jones is one of the clients who was chosen to represent the district.
   D. All are incorrect.

2. A. He is taller than I. 2.____
   B. I'll have nothing to do with these kind of people.
   C. The reason why he will not buy the house is because it is too expensive.
   D. All are incorrect.

3. A. Aren't I eligible for this apartment. 3.____
   B. Have you seen him anywheres?
   C. He should of come earlier.
   D. All are incorrect.

4. A. He graduated college in 2022. 4.____
   B. He hadn't but one more line to write.
   C. Who do you think is the author of this report?
   D. All are incorrect.

Questions 5-35.

DIRECTIONS: In each of the following questions, only one of the four sentences conforms to standards of correct usage. The other three contain errors in grammar, diction, or punctuation. Select the choice in each question which BEST conforms to standards of correct usage. Consider a choice correct if it contains none of the errors mentioned above, even though there may be other ways of expressing the same thought.

5. A. It is obvious that no one wants to be a kill-joy if they can help it. 5.____
   B. It is not always possible, and perhaps it never ispossible, to judge a person's character by just looking at him.
   C. When Yogi Berra of the New York Yankees hit an immortal grandslam home run, everybody in the huge stadium including Pittsburgh fans, rose to his feet.
   D. Every one of us students must pay tuition today.

6. A. The physician told the young mother that if the baby is not able to digest its milk, it should be boiled.
   B. There is no doubt whatsoever that he felt deeply hurt because John Smith had betrayed the trust.
   C. Having partaken of a most delicious repast prepared by Tessie Breen, the hostess, the horses were driven home immediately thereafter.
   D. The attorney asked my wife and myself several questions.

6.____

7. A. Despite all denials, there is no doubt in my mind that
   B. At this time everyone must deprecate the demogogic attack made by one of our Senators on one of our most revered statesmen.
   C. In the first game of a crucial two-game series, Ted Williams, got two singles, both of them driving in a run.
   D. Our visitor brought good news to John and I.

7.____

8. A. If he would have told me, I should have been glad to help him in his dire financial emergency.
   B. Newspaper men have often asserted that diplomats or so-called official spokesmen sometimes employ equivocation in attempts to deceive.
   C. I think someones coming to collect money for the Red Cross.
   D. In a masterly summation, the young attorney expressed his belief that the facts clearly militate against this opinion.

8.____

9. A. We have seen most all the exhibits.
   B. Without in the least underestimating your advice, in my opinion the situation has grown immeasurably worse in the past few days.
   C. I wrote to the box office treasurer of the hit show that a pair of orchestra seats would be preferable.
   D. As the grim story of Pearl Harbor was broadcast on that fateful December 7, it was the general opinion that war was inevitable.

9.____

10. A. Without a moment's hesitation, Casey Stengel said that Larry Berra works harder than any player on the team.
    B. There is ample evidence to indicate that many animals can run faster than any human being.
    C. No one saw the accident but I.
    D. Example of courage is the heroic defense put up by the paratroopers against overwhelming odds.

10.____

11. A. If you prefer these kind, Mrs. Grey, we shall be more than willing to let you have them reasonably.
    B. If you like these here, Mrs. Grey, we shall be more than willing to let you have them reasonably.
    C. If you like these, Mrs. Grey, we shall be more than willing to let you have them.
    D. Who shall we appoint?

11.____

12. A. The number of errors are greater in speech than in writing.
    B. The doctor rather than the nurse was to blame for his being neglected.
    C. Because the demand for these books have been so great, we reduced the price.
    D. John Galsworthy, the English novelist, could not have survived a serious illness; had it not been for loving care.

    12._____

13. A. Our activities this year have seldom ever been as interesting as they have been this month.
    B. Our activities this month have been more interesting, or at least as interesting as those of any month this year.
    C. Our activities this month has been more interesting than those of any other month this year.
    D. Neither Jean nor her sister was at home.

    13._____

14. A. George B. Shaw's view of common morality, as well as his wit sparkling with a dash of perverse humor here and there, have led critics to term him "The Incurable Rebel."
    B. The President's program was not always received with the wholehearted endorsement of his own party, which is why the party faces difficulty in drawing up a platform for the coming election.
    C. The reason why they wanted to travel was because they had never been away from home.
    D. Facing a barrage of cameras, the visiting celebrity found it extremely difficult to express his opinions clearly.

    14._____

15. A. When we calmed down, we all agreed that our anger had been kind of unnecessary and had not helped the situation.
    B. Without him going into all the details, he made us realize the horror of the accident.
    C. Like one girl, for example, who applied for two positions.
    D. Do not think that you have to be so talented as he is in order to play in the school orchestra.

    15._____

16. A. He looked very peculiarly to me.
    B. He certainly looked at me peculiar.
    C. Due to the train's being late, we had to wait an hour.
    D. The reason for the poor attendance is that it is raining.

    16._____

17. A. About one out of four own an automobile.
    B. The collapse of the old Mitchell Bridge was caused by defective construction in the central pier.
    C. Brooks Atkinson was well acquainted with the best literature, thus helping him to become an able critic.
    D. He has to stand still until the relief man comes up, thus giving him no chance to move about and keep warm.

    17._____

18. A. He is sensitive to confusion and withdraws from people whom he feels are too noisy.
    B. Do you know whether the data is statistically correct?
    C. Neither the mayor or the aldermen are to blame.
    D. Of those who were graduated from high school, a goodly percentage went to college.

18.____

19. A. Acting on orders, the offices were searched by a designated committee.
    B. The answer probably is nothing.
    C. I thought it to be all right to excuse them from class.
    D. I think that he is as successful a singer, if not more successful, than Mary.

19.____

20. A. $360,000 is really very little to pay for such a wellbuilt house.
    B. The creatures looked like they had come from outer space.
    C. It was her, he knew!
    D. Nobody but me knows what to do.

20.____

21. A. Mrs. Smith looked good in her new suit.
    B. New York may be compared with Chicago.
    C. I will not go to the meeting except you go with me.
    D. I agree with this editorial.

21.____

22. A. My opinions are different from his.
    B. There will be less students in class now.
    C. Helen was real glad to find her watch.
    D. It had been pushed off of her dresser.

22.____

23. A. Almost everyone, who has been to California, returns with glowing reports.
    B. George Washington, John Adams, and Thomas Jefferson, were our first presidents.
    C. Mr. Walters, whom we met at the bank yesterday, is the man, who gave me my first job.
    D. One should study his lessons as carefully as he can.

23.____

24. A. We had such a good time yesterday.
    B. When the bell rang, the boys and girls went in the schoolhouse.
    C. John had the worst headache when he got up this morning.
    D. Today's assignment is somewhat longer than yesterday's.

24.____

25. A. Neither the mayor nor the city clerk are willing to talk.
    B. Neither the mayor nor the city clerk is willing to talk.
    C. Neither the mayor or the city clerk are willing to talk.
    D  Neither the mayor or the city clerk is willing to talk.

25.____

26. A. Being that he is that kind of boy, cooperation cannot be expected.
    B. He interviewed people who he thought had something to say.
    C. Stop whomever enters the building regardless of rank or office held.
    D. Passing through the countryside, the scenery pleased us.

26.____

27. A. The childrens' shoes were in their closet.
    B. The children's shoes were in their closet.
    C. The childs' shoes were in their closet.
    D. The childs' shoes were in his closet.

28. A. An agreement was reached between the defendant, the plaintiff, the plaintiff's attorney and the insurance company as to the amount of the settlement.
    B. Everybody was asked to give their versions of the accident.
    C. The consensus of opinion was that the evidence was inconclusive.
    D. The witness stated that if he was rich, he wouldn't have had to loan the money.

29. A. Before beginning the investigation, all the materials related to the case were carefully assembled.
    B. The reason for his inability to keep the appointment is because of his injury in the accident.
    C. This here evidence tends to support the claim of the defendant.
    D. We interviewed all the witnesses who, according to the driver, were still in town.

30. A. Each claimant was allowed the full amount of their medical expenses.
    B. Either of the three witnesses is available.
    C. Every one of the witnesses was asked to tell his story.
    D. Neither of the witnesses are right.

31. A. The commissioner, as well as his deputy and various bureau heads, were present.
    B. A new organization of employers and employees have been formed.
    C. One or the other of these men have been selected.
    D. The number of pages in the book is enough to discourage a reader.

32. A. Between you and me, I think he is the better man.
    B. He was believed to be me.
    C. Is it us that you wish to see?
    D. The winners are him and her.

33. A. Beside the statement to the police, the witness spoke to no one.
    B. He made no statement other than to the police and I.
    C. He made no statement to any one else, aside from the police.
    D. The witness spoke to no one but me.

34. A. The claimant has no one to blame but himself.
    B. The boss sent us, he and I, to deliver the packages.
    C. The lights come from mine and not his car.
    D. There was room on the stairs for him and myself.

35. A. Admission to this clinic is limited to patients' inability to pay for medical care.
    B. Patients who can pay little or nothing for medical care are treated in this clinic.
    C. The patient's ability to pay for medical care is the determining factor in his admission to this clinic.
    D. This clinic is for the patient's that cannot afford to pay or that can pay a little for medical care.

35.____

# KEY (CORRECT ANSWERS)

| | | | | | | | |
|---|---|---|---|---|---|---|---|
| 1. | A | 11. | C | 21. | A | 31. | D |
| 2. | A | 12. | B | 22. | A | 32. | A |
| 3. | D | 13. | D | 23. | D | 33. | D |
| 4. | C | 14. | D | 24. | D | 34. | A |
| 5. | D | 15. | D | 25. | B | 35. | B |
| 6. | D | 16. | D | 26. | B | | |
| 7. | B | 17. | B | 27. | B | | |
| 8. | B | 18. | D | 28. | C | | |
| 9. | D | 19. | B | 29. | D | | |
| 10. | B | 20. | D | 30. | C | | |

# EXAMINATION SECTION
## TEST 1

DIRECTIONS: Each question or incomplete statement is followed by several suggested answers or completions. Select the one that BEST answers the question or completes the statement. *PRINT THE LETTER OF THE CORRECT ANSWER IN THE SPACE AT THE RIGHT.*

1. Which of the following sentences is punctuated INCORRECTLY?  1.____
   A. Johnson said, "One tiny virus, Blanche, can multiply so fast that it will become 200 viruses in 25 minutes."
   B. With economic pressures hitting them from all sides, American farmers have become the weak link in the food chain.
   C. The degree to which this is true, of course, depends on the personalities of the people involved, the subject matter, and the atmosphere in general.
   D. "What loneliness, asked George Eliot, is more lonely than distrust?"

2. Which of the following sentences is punctuated INCORRECTLY?  2.____
   A. Based on past experiences, do you expect the plumber to show up late, not have the right parts, and overcharge you.
   B. When polled, however, the participants were most concerned that it be convenient.
   C. No one mentioned the flavor of the coffee, and no one seemed to care that china was used instead of plastic.
   D. As we said before, sometimes people view others as things; they don't see them as living, breathing beings like themselves.

3. Convention members travelled here from Kingston New York Pittsfield Massachusetts Bennington Vermont and Hartford Connecticut.  3.____
   How many commas should there be in the above sentence?
   A. 3        B. 4        C. 5        D. 6

4. Of the two speakers the one who spoke about human rights is more famous and more humble.  4.____
   How many commas should there be in the above sentence?
   A. 1        B. 2        C. 3        D. 4

5. Which sentence is punctuated INCORRECTLY?  5.____
   A. Five people voted no; two voted yes; one person abstained.
   B. Well, consider what has been said here today, but we won't make any promises.
   C. Anthropologists divide history into three major periods: the Stone Age, the Bronze Age, and the Iron Age.
   D. Therefore, we may create a stereotype about people who are unsuccessful; we may see them as lazy, unintelligent, or afraid of success.

6. Which sentence is punctuated INCORRECTLY?  6._____
   A. Studies have found that the unpredictability of customer behavior can lead to a great deal of stress, particularly if the behavior is unpleasant or if the employee has little control over it.
   B. If this degree of emotion and variation can occur in spectator sports, imagine the role that perceptions can play when there are real stakes involved.
   C. At other times, however hidden expectations may sabotage or severely damage an encounter without anyone knowing what happened.
   D. There are usually four issues to look for in a conflict: differences in values, goals, methods, and facts.

Questions 7-10.

DIRECTIONS: Questions 7 through 10 test your ability to distinguish between words that sound alike but are spelled differently and have different meanings. In the following groups of sentences, one of the underlined words is used incorrectly.

7. A. By accepting responsibility for their actions, managers promote trust.  7._____
   B. Dropping hints or making illusions to things that you would like changed sometimes leads to resentment.
   C. The entire unit loses respect for the manager and resents the reprimand.
   D. Many people are averse to confronting problems directly; they would rather avoid them.

8. A. What does this say about the effect our expectations have on those we supervise?  8._____
   B. In an effort to save time between 9 A.M. and 1 P.M., the staff members devised their own interpretation of what was to be done on these forms.
   C. The taskmaster's principal concern is for getting the work done; he or she is not concerned about the need or interests of employees.
   D. The advisor's main objective was increasing Angela's ability to invest her capitol wisely.

9. A. A typical problem is that people have to cope with the internal censer of their feelings.  9._____
   B. Sometimes, in their attempt to sound more learned, people speak in ways that are barely comprehensible.
   C. The council will meet next Friday to decide whether Abrams should continue as representative.
   D. His descent from grace was assured by that final word.

10. A. The doctor said that John's leg had to remain stationary or it would not heal properly.  10._____
    B. There is a city ordinance against parking too close to fire hydrants.
    C. Meyer's problem is that he is never discrete when talking about office politics.
    D. Mrs. Thatcher probably worked harder than any other British Prime Minister had ever worked.

Questions 11-20.

DIRECTIONS: For each of the following groups of sentences in Questions 11 through 20, select the sentence which is the BEST example of English usage and grammar.

11.  A. She is a woman who, at age sixty, is distinctly attractive and cares about how they look.
     B. It was a seemingly impossible search, and no one knew the problems better than she.
     C. On the surface, they are all sweetness and light, but his morbid character is under it.
     D. The minicopier, designed to appeal to those who do business on the run like architects in the field or business travelers, weigh about four pounds.

11.____

12.  A. Neither the administrators nor the union representative regret the decision to settle the disagreement.
     B. The plans which are made earlier this year were no longer being considered.
     C. I would have rode with him if I had known he was leaving at five.
     D. I don't know who she said had it.

12.____

13.  A. Writing at a desk, the memo was handed to her for immediate attention.
     B. Carla didn't water Carl's plants this week, which she never does.
     C. Not only are they good workers, with excellent writing and speaking skills, and they get to the crux of any problem we hand them.
     D. We've noticed that this enthusiasm for undertaking new projects sometimes interferes with his attention to detail.

13.____

14.  A. It's obvious that Nick offends people by being unruly, inattentive, and having no patience.
     B. Marcia told Genie that she would have to leave soon.
     C. Here are the papers you need to complete your investigation.
     D. Julio was startled by you're comment.

14.____

15.  A. The new manager has done good since receiving her promotion, but her secretary has helped her a great deal.
     B. One of the personnel managers approached John and tells him that the client arrived unexpectedly.
     C. If somebody can supply us with the correct figures, they should do so immediately.
     D. Like zealots, advocates seek power because they want to influence the policies and actions of an organization.

15.____

16. A. Between you and me, Chris probably won't finish this assignment in time.                    16.____
    B. Rounding the corner, the snack bar appeared before us.
    C. Parker's radical reputation made to the Supreme Court his appointment impossible.
    D. By the time we arrived, Marion finishes briefing James and returns to Hank's office.

17. A. As we pointed out earlier, the critical determinant of the success of middle                 17.____
       managers is their ability to communicate well with others.
    B. The lecturer stated there wasn't no reason for bad supervision.
    C. We are well aware whose at fault in this instance.
    D. When planning important changes, it's often wise to seek the participation of others because employees often have much valuable ideas to offer.

18. A. Joan had ought to throw out those old things that were damaged when the                     18.____
       roof leaked.
    B. I spose he'll let us know what he's decided when he finally comes to a decision.
    C. Carmen was walking to work when she suddenly realized that she had left her lunch on the table as she passed the market.
    D. Are these enough plants for your new office?

19. A. First move the lever forward, and then they should lift the ribbon casing                   19.____
       before trying to take it out.
    B. Michael finished quickest than any other person in the office.
    C. There is a special meeting for we committee members today at 4 p.m.
    D. My husband is worried about our having to work overtime next week.

20. A. Another source of conflicts are individuals who possess very poor                            20.____
       interpersonal skills.
    B. It is difficult for us to work with him on projects because these kinds of people are not interested in team building.
    C. Each of the departments was represented at the meeting.
    D. Poor boy, he never should of past that truck on the right.

Questions 21-28.

DIRECTIONS:   In Questions 21 through 28, there may be a problem with English grammar or usage. If a problem does exist, select the letter that indicates the most effective change. If no problem exists, select Choice A.

21. He rushed her to the hospital and stayed with her, even though this took quite a               21.____
    bit of his time, he didn't charge her anything.
       A. No changes are necessary.
       B. Change even though to although
       C. Change the first comma to a period and capitalize even
       D. Change rushed to had rushed

22. Waiting that appears unfairly feels longer than waiting that seems justified.  22.____
    A. No changes are necessary.
    B. Change unfairly to unfair
    C. Change appears to seems
    D. Change longer to longest

23. May be you and the person who argued with you will be able to reach an agreement.  23.____
    A. No changes are necessary
    B. Change will be to were
    C. Change argued with to had an argument with
    D. Change May be to Maybe

24. Any one of them could of taken the file while you were having coffee.  24.____
    A. No changes are necessary
    B. Change any one to anyone
    C. Change of to have
    D. Change were having to were out having

25. While people get jobs or move from poverty level to better paying employment, they stop receiving benefits and start paying taxes.  25.____
    A. No changes are necessary
    B. Change While to As
    C. Change stop to will stop
    D. Change get to obtain

26. Maribeth's phone rang while talking to George about the possibility of their meeting Tom at three this afternoon.  26.____
    A. No changes are necessary
    B. Change their to her
    C. Move to George so that it follows Tom
    D. Change talking to she was talking

27. According to their father, Lisa is smarter than Chris, but Emily is the smartest of the three sisters.  27.____
    A. No changes are necessary
    B. Change their to her
    C. Change is to was
    D. Make two sentences, changing the second comma to a period and omitting but

28. Yesterday, Mark and he claim that Carl took Carol's ideas and used them inappropriately.  28.____
    A. No changes are necessary
    B. Change claim to claimed
    C. Change inappropriately to inappropriate
    D. Change Carol's to Carols'

Questions 29-34.

DIRECTIONS: For each group of sentences in Questions 29 through 34, select the choice that represents the BEST editing of the problem sentence.

29. The managers expected employees to be at their desks at all times, but they would always be late or leave unannounced.
    A. The managers wanted employees to always be at their desks, but they would always be late or leave unannounced.
    B. Although the managers expected employees to be at their desks no matter what came up, they would always be late and leave without telling anyone.
    C. Although the managers expected employees to be at their desks at all times, the managers would always be late or leave without telling anyone.
    D. The managers expected the employee to never leave their desks, but they would always be late or leave without telling anyone.

29.____

30. The one who is department manager he will call you to discuss the problem tomorrow morning at 10 A.M.
    A. The one who is department manager will call you tomorrow morning at ten to discuss the problem.
    B. The department manager will call you to discuss the problem tomorrow at 10 A.M.
    C. Tomorrow morning at 10 A.M., the department manager will call you to discuss the problem.
    D. Tomorrow morning the department manager will call you to discuss the problem.

30.____

31. A conference on child care in the workplace the $200 cost of which to attend may be prohibitive to childcare workers who earn less than that weekly.
    A. A conference on child care in the workplace that costs $200 may be too expensive for childcare workers who earn less than that each week.
    B. A conference on child care in the workplace, the cost of which to attend is $200, may be prohibitive to childcare workers who earn less than that weekly.
    C. A conference on child care in the workplace who costs $200 may be too expensive for childcare workers who earn less than that a week.
    D. A conference on child care in the workplace which costs $200 may be too expensive to childcare workers who earn less than that on a weekly basis.

31.____

32. In accordance with estimates recently made, there are 40,000 to 50,000 nuclear weapons in our world today.
    A. Because of estimates recently, there are 40,000 to 50,000 nuclear weapons in the world today.
    B. In accordance with estimates made recently, there are 40,000 to 50,000 nuclear weapons in the world today.

32.____

C. According to estimates made recently, there are 40,000 to 50,000 weapons in the world today.
D. According to recent estimates, there are 40,000 to 50,000 nuclear weapons in the world today.

33. Motivation is important in problem solving, but they say that excessive motivation can inhibit the creative process. 33.____
    A. Motivation is important in problem solving, but, as they say, too much of it can inhibit the creative process.
    B. Motivation is important in problem solving and excessive motivation will inhibit the creative process.
    C. Motivation is important in problem solving, but excessive motivation can inhibit the creative process.
    D. Motivation is important in problem solving because excessive motivation can inhibit the creative process.

34. In selecting the best option calls for consulting with all the people that are involved in it. 34.____
    A. In selecting the best option consulting with all people concerned with it.
    B. Calling for the best option, we consulted all the affected people.
    C. We called all the people involved to select the best option.
    D. To be sure of selecting the best option, one should consult all the people involved.

35. There are a number of problems with the following letter. From the options below, select the version that is MOST in accordance with standard business style, tone, and form. 35.____

Dear Sir:

   We are so sorry that we have had to backorder your order for 15,000 widgets and 2,300 whatzits for such a long time. We have been having incredibly bad luck lately. When your order first came in no one could get to it because my secretary was out with the flu and her replacement didn't know what she was doing, then there was the dock strike in Cucamonga which held things up for awhile, and then it just somehow got lost. We think it may have fallen behind the radiator.
   We are happy to say that all these problems have been taken care of, we are caught up on supplies, and we should have the stuff to you soon, in the near future—about two weeks. You may not believe us after everything you've been through with us, but it's true.
   We'll let you know as soon as we have a secure date for delivery. Thank you so much for continuing to do business with us after all the problems this probably has caused you.

Yours very sincerely,
Rob Barker

A. Dear Sir:

    We are so sorry that we have had to backorder your order for 15,000 widgets and 2,300 whatzits. We have been having problems with staff lately and the dock strike hasn't helped anything.
    We are happy to say that all these problems have been taken care of. I've told my secretary to get right on it, and we should have the stuff to you soon. Thank you so much for continuing to do business with us after all the problems this must have caused you.
    We'll let you know as soon as we have a secure date for delivery.

    Sincerely,
    Rob Barker

B. Dear Sir:

    We regret that we haven't been able to fill your order for 15,000 widgets and 2,300 whatzits in a timely fashion.
    We'll let you know as soon as we have a secure date for delivery.

    Sincerely,
    Rob Barker

C. Dear Sir:

    We are so very sorry that we haven't been able to fill your order for 15,000 widgets and 2,300 whatzits. We have been having incredibly bad luck lately, but things are much better now.
    Thank you so much for bearing with us through all of this. We'll let you know as soon as we have a secure date for delivery.

    Sincerely,
    Rob Barker

D. Dear Sir:

    We are very sorry that we haven't been able to fill your order for 15,000 widgets and 2,300 whatzits. Due to unforeseen difficulties, we have had to back-order your request. At this time, supplies have caught up to demand, and we foresee a delivery date within the next two weeks.
    We'll let you know as soon as we have a secure date for delivery. Thank you for your patience.

    Sincerely,
    Rob Barker

## KEY (CORRECT ANSWERS)

| | | | | | | | |
|---|---|---|---|---|---|---|---|
| 1. | D | 11. | B | 21. | C | 31. | A |
| 2. | A | 12. | D | 22. | B | 32. | D |
| 3. | B | 13. | D | 23. | D | 33. | C |
| 4. | A | 14. | C | 24. | C | 34. | D |
| 5. | B | 15. | D | 25. | B | 35. | D |
| 6. | C | 16. | A | 26. | D | | |
| 7. | B | 17. | A | 27. | A | | |
| 8. | D | 18. | D | 28. | B | | |
| 9. | A | 19. | D | 29. | C | | |
| 10. | C | 20. | C | 30. | B | | |

# NAME AND NUMBER COMPARISONS

## COMMENTARY

This test seeks to measure your ability and disposition to do a job carefully and accurately, your attention to exactness and preciseness of detail, your alertness and versatility in discerning similarities and differences between things, and your power in systematically handling written language symbols.

It is actually a test of your ability to do academic and/or clerical work, using the basic elements of verbal (qualitative) and mathematical (quantitative) learning—words and numbers.

# EXAMINATION SECTION

## TEST 1

DIRECTIONS: In each line across the page there are three names or numbers that are much alike. Compare the three names or numbers and decide which ones are exactly alike. *PRINT IN THE SPACE AT THE RIGHT THE LETTER:*
A. if all THREE names or numbers are exactly alike
B. if only the FIRST and SECOND names or numbers are ALIKE
C. if only the FIRST and THIRD names or numbers are alike
D. if only the SECOND or THIRD names or numbers are alike
E. if ALL THREE names or numbers are DIFFERENT

| | | | | | |
|---|---|---|---|---|---|
| 1. | Davis Hazen | David Hozen | David Hazen | | 1.____ |
| 2. | Lois Appel | Lois Appel | Lois Apfel | | 2.____ |
| 3. | June Allan | Jane Allan | Jane Allan | | 3.____ |
| 4. | 10235 | 10235 | 10235 | | 4.____ |
| 5. | 32614 | 32164 | 32614 | | 5.____ |

## TEST 2

| | | | | | |
|---|---|---|---|---|---|
| 1. | 2395890 | 2395890 | 2395890 | | 1.____ |
| 2. | 1926341 | 1926347 | 1926314 | | 2.____ |
| 3. | E. Owens McVey | E. Owen McVey | E. Owen McVay | | 3.____ |
| 4. | Emily Neal Rouse | Emily Neal Rowse | Emily Neal Rowse | | 4.____ |
| 5. | H. Merritt Audubon | H. Merriott Audubon | H. Merritt Audubon | | 5.____ |

## TEST 3

1. 6219354     6219354     6219354     1.\_\_\_\_
2. 231793     2312793     2312793     2.\_\_\_\_
3. 1065407     1065407     1065047     3.\_\_\_\_
4. Francis Ransdell     Frances Ramsdell     Francis Ramsdell     4.\_\_\_\_
5. Cornelius Detwiler     Cornelius Detwiler     Cornelius Detwiler     5.\_\_\_\_

## TEST 4

1. 6452054     6452564     6542054     1.\_\_\_\_
2. 8501268     8501268     8501286     2.\_\_\_\_
3. Ella Burk Newham     Ella Burk Newnham     Elena Burk Newnham     3.\_\_\_\_
4. Jno. K. Ravencroft     Jno. H. Ravencroft     Jno. H. Ravencoft     4.\_\_\_\_
5. Martin Wills Pullen     Martin Wills Pulen     Martin Wills Pullen     5.\_\_\_\_

## TEST 5

1. 3457988     3457986     3457986     1.\_\_\_\_
2. 4695682     4695862     4695682     2.\_\_\_\_
3. Stricklund Kaneydy     Sticklund Kanedy     Stricklund Kanedy     3.\_\_\_\_
4. Joy Harlor Witner     Joy Harloe Witner     Joy Harloe Witner     4.\_\_\_\_
5. R.M.O. Uberroth     R.M.O. Uberroth     R.N.O. Uberroth     5.\_\_\_\_

## TEST 6

| | | | |
|---|---|---|---|
| 1. 1592514 | 1592574 | 1592574 | 1._____ |
| 2. 2010202 | 2010202 | 2010220 | 2._____ |
| 3. 6177396 | 6177936 | 6177396 | 3._____ |
| 4. Drusilla S. Ridgeley | Drusilla S. Ridgeley | Drusilla S. Ridgeley | 4._____ |
| 5. Andrei I. Tooumantzev | Andrei I. Tourmantzev | Andrei I. Toumantzov | 5._____ |

## TEST 7

| | | | |
|---|---|---|---|
| 1. 5261383 | 5261383 | 5261338 | 1._____ |
| 2. 8125690 | 8126690 | 8125609 | 2._____ |
| 3. W.E. Johnston | W.E. Johnson | W.E. Johnson | 3._____ |
| 4. Vergil L. Muller | Vergil L. Muller | Vergil L. Muller | 4._____ |
| 5. Atherton R. Warde | Asheton R. Warde | Atherton P. Warde | 5._____ |

## TEST 8

| | | | |
|---|---|---|---|
| 1. 013469.5 | 023469.5 | 02346.95 | 1._____ |
| 2. 33376 | 333766 | 333766 | 2._____ |
| 3. Ling-Temco-Vought | Ling-Tenco-Vought | Ling-Temco Vought | 3._____ |
| 4. Lorilard Corp. | Lorillard Corp. | Lorrilard Corp. | 4._____ |
| 5. American Agronomics Corporation | American Agronomics Corporation | American Agronomic Corporation | 5._____ |

## TEST 9

1. 436592864                          436592864                          436592864                          1.____

2. 197765123                          197755123                          197755123                          2.____

3. Dewaay Cortvriendt          Deway Cortvriendt           Deway Corturiendt           3.____
   International S.A.              International S.A.              International S.A.

4. Crédit Lyonnais                  Crèdit Lyonnais                 Crèdit Lyonais                  4.____

5. Algemene Bank              Algamene Bank              Algemene Bank              5.____
   Nederland N.V.                 Nederland N.V.                 Naderland N.V.

## TEST 10

1. 00032572                           0.0032572                          00032522                           1.____

2. 399745                              399745                               398745                              2.____

3. Banca Privata                   Banca Privata                   Banca Privata                   3.____
   Finanziaria S.p.A.             Finanzaria S.P.A.              Finanziaria S.P.A.

4. Eastman Dillon,               Eastman Dillon,               Eastman Dillon,               4.____
   Union Securities & Co.    Union Securities Co.       Union Securities & Co.

5. Arnhold and S.                  Arnhold & S.                      Arnold and S.                    5.____
   Bleichroeder, Inc.             Bleichroeder, Inc.             Bleichroeder, Inc.

# TEST 11

DIRECTIONS: Answer the questions below on the basis of the following instructions: For each such numbered set of names, addresses, and numbers listed in Columns I and II, select your answer from the following options:
A. The names in Columns I and II are different
B. The addresses in Columns I and II are different
C. The numbers in Columns I and II are different
D. The names, addresses and numbers are identical

1. Francis Jones
62 Stately Avenue
96-12446

    Francis Jones
62 Stately Avenue
96-21446

    1.____

2. Julio Montez
19 Ponderosa Road
56-73161

    Julio Montez
19 Ponderosa Road
56-71361

    2.____

3. Mary Mitchell
2314 Melbourne Drive
68-92172

    Mary Mitchell
2314 Melbourne Drive
68-92172

    3.____

4. Harry Patterson
25 Dunne Street
14-33430

    Harry Patterson
25 Dunne Street
14-34330

    4.____

5. Patrick Murphy
171 West Hosmer Street
93-81214

    Patrick Murphy
171 West Hosmer Street
93-18214

    5.____

# TEST 12

1. August Schultz
   816 St. Clair Avenue
   53-40149

   August Schultz
   816 St. Claire Avenue
   53-40149

   1.____

2. George Taft
   72 Runnymede Street
   47-04033

   George Taft
   72 Runnymede Street
   47-04023

   2.____

3. Angus Henderson
   1418 Madison Street
   81-76375

   Angus Henderson
   1418 Madison Street
   81-76375

   3.____

4. Carolyn Mazur
   12 Rivenlew Road
   38-99615

   Carolyn Mazur
   12 Rivervane Road
   38-99615

   4.____

5. Adele Russell
   1725 Lansing Lane
   72-91962

   Adela Russell
   1725 Lansing Lane
   72-91962

   5.____

# TEST 13

DIRECTIONS: The following questions are based on the instructions given below. In each of the following questions, the 3-line name and address in Column I is the masterlist entry, and the 3-line entry in Column II is the information to be checked against the master list.
If there is one line that is NOT exactly alike, mark your answer A.
If there are two lines NOT exactly alike, mark your answer B.
If there are three lines NOT exactly alike, mark your answer C.
If the lines ALL are exactly alike, mark your answer D.

1. Jerome A. Jackson
   1243 14th Avenue
   New York, N.Y. 10023

   Jerome A. Johnson
   1234 14th Avenue
   New York, N.Y. 10023

   1.____

2. Sophie Strachtheim
   33-28 Connecticut Ave.
   Far Rockaway, N.Y. 11697

   Sophie Strachtheim
   33-28 Connecticut Ave.
   Far Rockaway, N.Y. 11697

   2.____

3. Elisabeth NT. Gorrell
   256 Exchange St
   New York, N.Y. 10013

   Elizabeth NT. Correll
   256 Exchange St.
   New York, N.Y. 10013

   3.____

4. Maria J. Gonzalez
   7516 E. Sheepshead Rd.
   Brooklyn, N.Y. 11240

   Maria J. Gonzalez
   7516 N. Shepshead Rd.
   Brooklyn, N.Y. 11240

   4.____

5. Leslie B. Brautenweiler
   21-57A Seller Terr.
   Flushing, N.Y. 11367

   Leslie B. Brautenwieler
   21-75ASeiler Terr.
   Flushing, N.J. 11367

   5.____

## KEY (CORRECT ANSWERS)

| TEST 1 | TEST 2 | TEST 3 | TEST 4 | TEST 5 | TEST 6 | TEST 7 |
|--------|--------|--------|--------|--------|--------|--------|
| 1. E | 1. A | 1. A | 1. E | 1. D | 1. D | 1. B |
| 2. B | 2. E | 2. A | 2. B | 2. C | 2. B | 2. E |
| 3. D | 3. E | 3. B | 3. E | 3. E | 3. C | 3. D |
| 4. A | 4. D | 4. E | 4. E | 4. D | 4. A | 4. A |
| 5. C | 5. C | 5. A | 5. C | 5. B | 5. E | 5. E |

| TEST 8 | TEST 9 | TEST 10 | TEST 11 | TEST 12 | TEST 13 |
|--------|--------|---------|---------|---------|---------|
| 1. E | 1. A | 1. E | 1. C | 1. B | 1. B |
| 2. D | 2. D | 2. B | 2. C | 2. C | 2. D |
| 3. E | 3. E | 3. E | 3. D | 3. D | 3. A |
| 4. E | 4. E | 4. C | 4. C | 4. B | 4. A |
| 5. B | 5. E | 5. E | 5. C | 5. A | 5. C |

# NAME AND NUMBER COMPARISONS

## COMMENTARY

This test seeks to measure your ability and disposition to do a job carefully and accurately, your attention to exactness and preciseness of detail, your alertness and versatility in discerning similarities and differences between things, and your power in systematically handling written language symbols.

It is actually a test of your ability to do academic and/or clerical work, using the basic elements of verbal (qualitative) and mathematical (quantitative) learning—words and numbers.

## EXAMINATION SECTION

## TEST 1

DIRECTIONS: Questions 1 through 6 consist of sets of names and addresses. In each question, the name and address in Column II should be an exact copy of the name and address in Column II. *PRINT IN THE SPACE AT THE RIGHT THE LETTER*
- A. if there is a mistake only in the name
- B. if there is a mistake only in the address
- C. if there is a mistake in both name and address
- D. If there is no mistake in either name or address

SAMPLE:
Michael Filbert
456 Reade Street
New York, N.Y. 10013

Michael Filbert
644 Reade Street
New York, N.Y. 10013

Since there is a mistake only in the address, the answer is B.

1. Esta Wong
141 West 68 St.
New York, N.Y. 10023

    Esta Wang
141 West 68 St.
New York, N.Y. 10023

    1._____

2. Dr. Alberto Grosso
3475 12th Avenue
Brooklyn, N.Y. 11218

    Dr. Alberto Grosso
3475 12th Avenue
Brooklyn, N.Y. 11218

    2._____

3. Mrs. Ruth Bortlas
482 Theresa Ct.
Far Rockaway, N.Y. 11691

    Ms. Ruth Bortias
482 Theresa Ct.
Far Rockaway, N.Y. 11169

    3._____

4. Mr. and Mrs. Howard Fox
2301 Sedgwick Ave.
Bronx, N.Y. 10468

    Mr. and Mrs. Howard Fox
231 Sedgwick Ave.
Bronx, N.Y. 10468

    4._____

5. Miss Marjorie Black
223 East 23 Street
New York, N.Y. 10010

    Miss Margorie Black
223 East 23 Street
New York, N.Y. 10010

    5._____

2 (#1)

6. Michelle Herman         Michelle Hermann         6.____
   806 Valley Rd.          806 Valley Dr.
   Old Tappan, N.J. 07675  Old Tappan, N.J. 07675

---

## KEY (CORRECT ANSWERS)

1. A
2. D
3. C
4. B
5. A
6. C

---

# TEST 2

DIRECTIONS: Questions 1 through 6 consist of sets of names and addresses. In each question, the name and address in Column II should be an exact copy of the name and address in Column II. *PRINT IN THE SPACE AT THE RIGHT THE LETTER*
- A. if there is a mistake only in the name
- B. if there is a mistake only in the address
- C. if there is a mistake in both name and address
- D. If there is no mistake in either name or address

1. Ms. Joan Kelly
313 Franklin Ave.
Brooklyn, N.Y. 11202

    Ms. Joan Kielly
    318 Franklin Ave.
    Brooklyn, N.Y. 11202

    1.____

2. Mrs. Eileen Engel
47-24 86 Road
Queens, N.Y. 11122

    Mrs. Ellen Engel
    47-24 86 Road
    Queens, N.Y. 11122

    2.____

3. Marcia Michaels
213 E. 81 St.
New York, N.Y. 10012

    Marcia Michaels
    213 E. 81 St.
    New York, N.Y. 10012

    3.____

4. Rev. Edward J. Smyth
1401 Brandeis Street
San Francisco, Calif. 96201

    Rev. Edward J. Smyth
    1401 Brandies Street
    San Francisco, Calif. 96201

    4.____

5. Alicia Rodriguez
24-68 81 St.
Elmhurst, N.Y. 11122

    Alicia Rodriquez
    2468 81 St.
    Elmhurst, N.Y. 11122

    5.____

6. Ernest Eissemann
21 Columbia St.
New York, N.Y. 10007

    Ernest Eisermann
    21 Columbia St.
    New York, N.Y. 10007

    6.____

## KEY (CORRECT ANSWERS)

1. C
2. A
3. D
4. B
5. C
6. A

# TEST 3

DIRECTIONS: Questions 1 through 8 consist of names, locations, and telephone numbers. In each question, the name, location and number in Column II should be an exact copy of the name, location, and number in Column I. *PRINT IN THE SPACE AT THE RIGHT THE LETTER*
    A. if there is a mistake in one line only
    B. if there is a mistake in two lines only
    C. if there is a mistake in three lines only
    D. if there are no mistakes in any of the lines

1. Ruth Lang
EAM Bldg., Room C101
625-2000, ext. 765

   Ruth Lang
EAM Bldg., Room C110
625-2000, ext. 765
   1.____

2. Anne Marie Ionozzi
Investigations, Room 827
576-4000, ext. 832

   Anna Marie Ionozzi
Investigation, Room 827
566-4000, ext. 832
   2.____

3. Willard Jameson
Fm C Bldg. Room 687
454-3010

   Willard Jamieson
Fm C Bldg. Room 687
454-3010
   3.____

4. Joanne Zimmermann
Bldg. SW, Room 314
532-4601

   Joanne Zimmermann
Bldg. SW, Room 314
532-4601
   4.____

5. Carlyle Whetstone
Payroll Division-A, Room 212A
262-5000, ext. 471

   Caryle Whetstone
Payroll Division-A, Room 212A
262-5000, ext. 417
   5.____

6. Kenneth Chiang
Legal Council, Room 9745
(201) 416-9100, ext. 17

   Kenneth Chiang
Legal Counsel, Room 9745
(201) 416-9100, ext. 17
   6.____

7. Ethel Koenig
Personnel Services Div, Rm 433
635-7572

   Ethel Hoenig
Personal Services Div, Rm 433
635-7527
   7.____

8. Joyce Ehrhardt
Office of Administrator, Rm W56
387-8706

   Joyce Ehrhart
Office of Administrator, Rm W56
387-7806
   8.____

## KEY (CORRECT ANSWERS)

1. A    6. A
2. C    7. C
3. A    8. B
4. D
5. B

# TEST 4

DIRECTIONS: Each of Questions 1 through 10 gives the identification number and name of a person who has received treatment at a certain hospital. You are to choose the option (A, B, C, or D) which has EXACTLY the same number and name as those given in the question.

SAMPLE QUESTION:
123765  Frank Y. Jones
   A. 123675  Frank Y. Jones
   B. 123765  Frank T. Jones
   C. 123765  Frank Y. Jones
   D. 123765  Frank Y. Jones

The correct answer is D, because it is the only option showing the identification number and name exactly as they are in the sample question.

1. 754898  Diane Malloy
   A. 745898  Diane Malloy      B. 754898  Dion Malloy
   C. 754898  Diane Malloy     D. 754898  Diane Maloy

2. 661818  Ferdinand Figueroa
   A. 661818  Ferdinand Figueroa   B. 661618  Ferdinand Figueroa
   C. 661818  Ferdnand Figueroa    D. 661818  Ferdinand Figueroa

3. 100101  Norman D. Braustein
   A. 100101  Norman D. Braustein  B. 101001  Norman D. Braustein
   C. 100101  Norman P. Braustien  D. 100101  Norman D. Bruastein

4. 838696  Robert Kittredge
   A. 838969  Robert Kittredge    B. 838696  Robert Kittredge
   C. 388696  Robert Kittredge    D. 838696  Robert Kittridge

5. 243716  Abraham Soletsky
   A. 243716  Abrahm Soletsky    B. 243716  Abraham Solestky
   C. 243176  Abraham Soletsky   D. 243716  Abraham Soletsky

6. 981121  Phillip M. Maas
   A. 981121  Phillip M. Mass     B. 981211  Phillip M. Maas
   C. 981121  Phillip M. Maas     D. 981121  Phillip N. Maas

7. 786556  George Macalusso
   A. 785656  George Macalusso   B. 786556  George Macalusso
   C. 786556  George Maculusso   D. 786556  George Macluasso

8. 639472  Eugene Weber
   A. 639472  Eugene Weber     B. 639472  Eugene Webre
   C. 693472  Eugene Weber     D. 639742  Eugene Weber

9.  724936  John J. Lomonaco
    A. 724936  John J. Lomanoco
    C. 7224936  John J. Lomonaco
    B. 724396  John L. Lomonaco
    D. 724936  John J. Lamonaco

    9.____

10. 899868  Michael Schnitzer
    A. 899868  Micheal Schnitzer
    C. 899688  Michael Schnitzer
    B. 898968  Michael Schnizter
    D. 899868  Michael Schnitzer

    10.____

# KEY (CORRECT ANSWERS)

1. C  6. C
2. D  7. B
3. A  8. A
4. B  9. C
5. D  10. D

# ARITHMETICAL COMPUTATION AND REASONING
## EXAMINATION SECTION
### TEST 1

DIRECTIONS: Each question or incomplete statement is followed by several suggested answers or completions. Select the one that BEST answers the question or completes the statement. *PRINT THE LETTER OF THE CORRECT ANSWER IN THE SPACE AT THE RIGHT.*

1. 3/8 less than $40 is 1.____
   A. $25      B. $65      C. $15      D. $55

2. 27/64 expressed as a percent is 2.____
   A. 40.625%  B. 42.188%  C. 43.750%  D. 45.313%

3. 1/6 more than 36 gross is _____ gross. 3.____
   A. 6        B. 48       C. 30       D. 42

4. 15 is 20% of 4.____

5. The number which when increased by 1/3 of itself equals 96 is 5.____
   A. 128      B. 72       C. 64       D. 32

6. 0.16 3/4 written as percent is 6.____
   A. 16 3/4%  B. 16.3/4%  C. .016 3/4%  D. .0016 3/4%

7. 55% of 15 is 7.____
   A. 82.5     B. 0.825    C. 0.0825   D. 8.25

8. The number which when decreased by 1/3 of itself equals 96 is 8.____
   A. 64       B. 32       C. 128      D. 144

9. A carpenter used a board 15 3/4 ft. long from which 3 footstools were made with sufficient lumber left over for half of another footstool. If the lumber cost 24 1/2¢ per foot, the cost of EACH footstool was 9.____
   A. $1.54    B. $3.86    C. $1.10    D. $1.08

10. In one year, a luncheonette purchased 1231 gallons of milk for $907.99. The AVERAGE cost per half pint was 10.____
    A. $0.046  B. $0.045   C. $0.047   D. $0.044

11. The product of 23 and 9 3/4 is 11.____
    A. 191 2/3  B. 224 1/4  C. 213 3/4  D. 32 3/4

12. An order for 345 machine bolts at $4.15 per hundred will cost 12.____
    A. $0.1432  B. $1.1432  C. $14.32   D. $143.20

13. The fractional equivalent of .0625 is

    A. 1/16    B. 1/15    C. 1/14    D. 1/13

14. The number 0.03125 equals

    A. 3/64    B. 1/16    C. 1/64    D. 1/32

15. 21.70 divided by 1.75 equals

    A. 124    B. 12.4    C. 1.24    D. .124

16. The average cost of school lunches for 100 children varied as follows: Monday, $0.285; Tuesday, $0.237; Wednesday, $0.264; Thursday, $0.276; Friday, $0.292. The AVERAGE lunch cost

    A. $0.136    B. $0.270    C. $0.135    D. $0.271

17. The cost of 5 dozen eggs at $8.52 per gross is

    A. $3.50    B. $42.60    C. $3.55    D. $3.74

18. 410.07 less 38.49 equals

    A. 372.58    B. 371.58    C. 381.58    D. 382.68

19. The cost of 7 3/4 tons of coal at $20.16 per ton is

    A. $15.12    B. $151.20    C. $141.12    D. $156.24

20. The sum of 90.79, 79.09, 97.90, and 9.97 is

    A. 277.75    B. 278.56    C. 276.94    D. 277.93

## KEY (CORRECT ANSWERS)

| | | | |
|---|---|---|---|
| 1. A | | 11. B | |
| 2. B | | 12. C | |
| 3. D | | 13. A | |
| 4. C | | 14. D | |
| 5. B | | 15. B | |
| 6. A | | 16. D | |
| 7. D | | 17. C | |
| 8. D | | 18. B | |
| 9. C | | 19. D | |
| 10. A | | 20. A | |

## SOLUTIONS TO PROBLEMS

1. ($40)(5/8) = $25

2. 27/64 = .421875 ≈ 42.188%

3. (36)(1 1/6) = 42

4. Let x = missing number. Then, 15 = .20x. Solving, x = 75

5. Let x = missing number. Then, x + 1/3 x = 96. Simplifying, 4/3 x = 96. Solving, x = 96 ÷ 4/3 = 72

6. .16 3/4 = 16 3/4% by simply moving the decimal point two places to the right.

7. (.55)(15) = 8.25

8. Let x = missing number. Then, x - 1/3 x = 96. Simplifying, 2/3 x = 96. Solving, x = 96 ÷ 2/3 = 144

9. 15 3/4 ÷ 3 1/2 = 4.5 feet per footstool. The cost of one footstool is ($.245)(4.5) = $1.1025 ≈ $1.10

10. $907.99 ÷ 1231 = $.7376 per gallon. Since there are 16 half-pints in a gallon, the average cost per half-pint is $.7376 ÷ 16 ≈ $.046

11. (23)(9 3/4) = (23)(9.75) = 224.25 or 224 1/4

12. ($4.15)(3.45) = $14.3175 = $14.32

13. .0625 = 625/10,000 = 1/16

14. .03125 = 3125/100,000 = 1/32

15. 21.70 ÷ 1.75 = 12.4

16. The sum of these lunches is $1.354. Then, $1.354 ÷ 5 = $.2708 = $.271

17. $8.52 ÷ 12 = $.71 per dozen. Then, the cost of 5 dozen is ($.71)(5) = $3.55

18. 410.07 - 38.49 = 371.58

19. ($20.16)(7.75) = $156.24

20. 90.79 + 79.09 + 97.90 + 9.97 = 277.75

# TEST 2

DIRECTIONS: Each question or incomplete statement is followed by several suggested answers or completions. Select the one that BEST answers the question or completes the statement. *PRINT THE LETTER OF THE CORRECT ANSWER IN THE SPACE AT THE RIGHT.*

1. 1600 is 40% of what number?

    A. 6400  B. 3200  C. 4000  D. 5600

2. An executive's time card reads: Arrived 9:15 A.M., Left 2:05 P.M. How many hours was he in the office? _____ hours _____ minutes.

    A. 5; 10  B. 4; 50  C. 4; 10  D. 5; 50

3. .4266 times .3333 will have the following number of decimals in the product:

    A. 8  B. 4  C. 1  D. None of these

4. An office floor is 25 ft. wide by 36 ft. long. To cover this floor with carpet will require _____ square yards.

    A. 100  B. 300  C. 900  D. 25

5. 1/8 of 1% expressed as a decimal is

    A. .125  B. .0125  C. 1.25  D. .00125

6. $\dfrac{6 \div 4}{6 \times 4}$ equals 6x4

    A. 1/16  B. 1  C. 1/6  D. 1/4

7. 1/25 of 230 equals

    A. 92.0  B. 9.20  C. .920  D. 920

8. 4 times 3/8 equals

    A. 1 3/8  B. 3/32  C. 12.125  D. 1.5

9. 3/4 divided by 4 equals

    A. 3  B. 3/16  C. 16/3  D. 16

10. 6/7 divided by 2/7 equals

    A. 6  B. 12/49  C. 3  D. 21

11. The interest on $240 for 90 days ' 6% is

    A. $4.80  B. $3.40  C. $4.20  D. $3.60

12. 16 2/3% of 1728 is

    A. 91  B. 288  C. 282  D. 280

13. 6 1/4% of 6400 is    13._____
    A. 2500    B. 410    C. 108    D. 400

14. 12 1/2% of 560 is    14._____
    A. 65    B. 40    C. 50    D. 70

15. 2 yards divided by 3 equals    15._____
    A. 2 feet    B. 1/2 yard    C. 3 yards    D. 3 feet

16. A school has 540 pupils. 45% are boys. How many girls are there in this school?    16._____
    A. 243    B. 297    C. 493    D. 394

17. .1875 is equivalent to    17._____
    A. 18 3/4    B. 75/18    C. 18/75    D. 3/16

18. A kitchen cabinet listed at $42 is sold for $33.60. The discount allowed is    18._____
    A. 10%    B. 15%    C. 20%    D. 30%

19. 3 6/8 divided by 8 1/4 equals    19._____
    A. 9 1/8    B. 12    C. 5/11    D. 243.16

20. An agent sold goods to the amount of $1480. His commission at 5 1/2% was    20._____
    A. $37.50    B. $81.40    C. 76.70    D. $81.10

---

## KEY (CORRECT ANSWERS

1. C    11. D
2. B    12. B
3. A    13. D
4. A    14. D
5. D    15. A

6. A    16. B
7. B    17. D
8. D    18. C
9. B    19. C
10. C   20. B

3 (#2)

# SOLUTIONS TO PROBLEMS

1. Let x = missing number. Then, 1600 = .40x. Solving, x = 4000

2. 2:05 PM - 9:15 AM = 4 hours 50 minutes

3. The product of two 4-decimal numbers is an 8-decimal number.

4. (25 ft)(36 ft) = 900 sq.ft. = 100 sq.yds.

5. (1/8)(1%) = (.125)(.01) = .00125

6. (6 ÷ 4) ÷ (6 x 4) = 3/2 ÷ 24 = (3/2)(1/24)= (1/16)

7. (1/25)(230) = 9.20

8. (4)(3/8) = 12/8 = 1.5

9. 3/4 ÷ 4 = (3/4)(1/4) = 3/16

10. 6/7 / 2/7 = (6/7)(7/2) = 3

11. ($240)(.06)(90/360) = $3.60

12. (16 2/3%)(1728) = (1/6)(1728) = 288

13. (6 1/4%)(6400) = (1/16)(6400) = 400

14. (12 1/2%)(560) = (1/8)(560) = 70

15. 2 yds ÷ 3 = 2/3 yds = (2/3)(3) = 2 ft.

16. If 45% are boys, then 55% are girls. Thus, (540)(.55) = 297

17. .1875 = 1875/10,000 = 3/16

18. $42 - $33.60 = $8.40.
    The discount is $8.40 ÷ $42 = .20 = 20%

19. 3 6/8 - 8 1/4 = (30/8)(4/33) = 5/11

20. ($1480)(.055) = $81.40

# TEST 3

DIRECTIONS: Each question or incomplete statement is followed by several suggested answers or completions. Select the one that BEST answers the question or completes the statement. *PRINT THE LETTER OF THE CORRECT ANSWER IN THE SPACE AT THE RIGHT.*

1. 93.648 divided by 0.4 is 1.____

   A. 23.412     B. 234.12     C. 2.3412     D. 2341.2

2. Add 4.3682, .0028, 34., 9.92, and from the sum subtract 1.992. 2.____
   The remainder is

   A. .46299     B. 4.6299     C. 462.99     D. 46.299

3. At $2.88 per gross, three dozen will cost 3.____

   A. $8.64      B. $0.96      C. $0.72      D. $11.52

4. 13 times 2.39 times 0.024 equals 4.____

   A. 745.68     B. 74.568     C. 7.4568     D. .74568

5. A living room suite is marked $64 less 25 percent. A cash discount of 10 percent is 5.____
   allowed.
   The cash price is

   A. $53.20     B. $47.80     C. $36.00     D. $43.20

6. 1/8 of 1 percent expressed as a decimal is 6.____

   A. .125       B. .0125      C. 1.25       D. .00125

7. 16 percent of 482.11 equals 7.____

   A. 77.1376    B. 771.4240   C. 7714.2400  D. 7.71424

8. A merchant sold a chair for $60. This was at a profit of 25 percent of what it cost him. 8.____
   The chair cost him

   A. $48        B. $45        C. $15        D. $75

9. Add 5 hours 13 minutes, 3 hours 49 minutes, and 14 minutes. The sum is _____ hours 9.____
   _____ minutes.

   A. 9; 16      B. 9;76       C. 8;16       D. 8;6

10. 89 percent of $482 is 10.____

    A. $428.98   B. $472.36    C. $42.90     D. $47.24

11. 200 percent of 800 is 11.____

    A. 16        B. 1600       C. 2500       D. 4

12. Add 2 feet 3 inches, 4 feet 11 inches, 8 inches, 6 feet 6 inches. 12.____
    The sum is _____ feet _____ inches.

    A. 12; 4     B. 12; 14     C. 14; 4      D. 14; 28

79

13. A merchant bought dresses at $15 each and sold them at $20 each. His overhead expenses are 20 percent of cost. His net profit on each dress is

    A. $1    B. $2    C. $3    D. $4

    13.____

14. 0.0325 expressed as a percent is

    A. 325%    B. 3 1/4%    C. 32 1/2%    D. 32.5%

    14.____

15. Add 3/4, 1/8, 1/32, 1/2; and from the sum subtract 4/8. The remainder is

    A. 2/32    B. 7/8    C. 29/32    D. 3/4

    15.____

16. A salesman gets a commission of 4 percent on his sales. If he wants his commission to amount to $40, he will have to sell merchandise totaling

    A. $160    B. $10    C. $1,000    D. $100

    16.____

17. Jones borrowed $225,000 for five years at 3 1/2 percent. The annual interest charge was

    A. $1,575    B. $1,555    C. $7,875    D. $39,375

    17.____

18. A kitchen cabinet listed at $42 is sold for $33.60. The discount allowed is _____ percent.

    A. 10    B. 15    C. 20    D. 30

    18.____

19. The exact number of days from May 5, 2007 to July 1, 2007 is _____ days.

    A. 59    B. 58    C. 56    D. 57

    19.____

20. A dealer sells an article at a loss of 50% of the cost. Based on the selling price, the loss is

    A. 25%    B. 50%    C. 100%    D. none of these

    20.____

# KEY (CORRECT ANSWERS)

| | | | |
|---|---|---|---|
| 1. | B | 11. | B |
| 2. | D | 12. | C |
| 3. | C | 13. | B |
| 4. | D | 14. | B |
| 5. | D | 15. | C |
| 6. | D | 16. | C |
| 7. | A | 17. | C |
| 8. | A | 18. | C |
| 9. | A | 19. | D |
| 10. | A | 20. | C |

# SOLUTIONS TO PROBLEMS

1. $93.648 \div .4 = 234.12$

2. $4.368 + .0028 + 34 + 9.92 - 1.992 = 48.291 - 1.992 = 46.299$

3. $2.88 for 12 dozen means $.24 per dozen. Three dozen will cost $(3)(\$.24) = \$.72$

4. $(13)(2.39)(.024) = .74568$

5. $(\$64)(.75)(.90) = \$43.20$

6. $(1/8)(1\%) = (.125)(.01) = .00125$

7. $(.16)(482.11) = 77.1376$

8. Let $x$ = cost. Then, $1.25x = \$60$. Solving, $x = \$48$

9. 5 hrs. 13 min. + 3 hrs. 49 min. + 14 min = 8 hrs. 76 min.

10. $(.89)(\$482) = \$428.98$

11. $200\% = 2$. So, $(200\%)(800) = (2)(800) = 1600$

12. 2 ft. 3 in. + 4 ft. 11 in. + 8 in. + 6 ft. 6 in. + 12 ft. 28 in. = 14 ft. 4 in.

13. Overhead is $(.20)(\$15) = \$3$. The net profit is $\$20 - \$15 - \$3 = \$2$

14. $.0325 = 3.25\% = 3\ 1/4\%$

15. $3/4 + 1/8 + 1/32 + 1/2 - 4/8 = 45/32 - 4/8 = 29/32$

16. Let $x$ = sales. Then, $\$40 = .04x$. Solving, $x = \$1000$

17. Annual interest is $(\$225,000)(.035) \times 1 = 7875$

18. $\$42 - \$33.60 = \$8.40$. Then, $\$8.40 \div \$42 = .20 = 20\%$

19. The number of days left for May, June, July is 26, 30, and 1. Thus, $26 + 30 + 1 = 57$

20. Let $x$ = cost, so that $.50x$ = selling price. The loss is represented by $.50x \div .50x = 1 = 100\%$ on the selling price. (Note: The loss in dollars is $x - .50x = .50x$)

# ARITHMETIC

# EXAMINATION SECTION

## TEST 1

DIRECTIONS: Each question or incomplete statement is followed by several suggested answers or completions. Select the one that BEST answers the question or completes the statement. *PRINT THE LETTER OF THE CORRECT ANSWER IN THE SPACE AT THE RIGHT.*

1. The result of a computation using only the numbers 8 and 7 is 15. In this computation, the number 15 is the
   A. product  B. sum  C. quotient
   D. difference  E. average

   1._____

2. Which statement describes how to find the average of a group of scores?
   A. Find the sum of the scores and divide by 2.
   B. Find the sum of the scores and divide by the number of scores.
   C. Arrange the scores from lowest to highest and select the middle one.
   D. Take half the difference between the highest score and the lowest score.
   E. None of the above

   2._____

3. 6428
   974
   86
   7280
   763
   5407

   A. 19,838  B. 20,828  C. 20,838  D. 20,928  E. 20,938

   3._____

4. What is the inverse operation used to check division?
   A. Addition  B. Subtraction  C. Multiplication
   D. Division  E. None of the above

   4._____

5. What is the ratio of 1 inch to 1 yard?
   A. 1  B. 3  C. 12  D. 24  E. 36

   5._____

6. Which of the following is NOT evenly divisible by 8?
   A. 6  B. 8  C. 40  D. 72  4. 104

   6._____

7. Each of the numerals listed below represents a number of feet. Which numeral MOST NEARLY represents the height of an average American man?
   A. .059  B. 0.59  C. 5.90  D. 59.0  E. 590

   7._____

Questions 8-9.

DIRECTIONS: Questions 8 and 9 are to be answered on the basis of the following line.

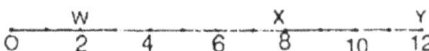

8. The point halfway between W and X would correspond to  8.____
   A. 4   B. 4 ½   C. 5   D. 5 ½   E. 6

9. What number would correspond to point P if it is placed on the number line  9.____
   so that P is between X and Y, and W is between P and X?
   A. 6
   B. 7 ½
   C. 9
   D. 10
   E. No such point can exist

10. What is the GREATEST common divisor of 24, 40, and 120?  10.____
    A. 2   B. 4   C. 8   D. 10   E. 12

11. Which of these is NOT equal to 4/9?  11.____
    A. 2/3   B. 20/45   C. 8/18   D. 16/36   E. 12/27

12. For which pair of the following operations are the rules for placing the  12.____
    decimal point in the answer the SAME?
    I. Addition              II. Subtraction
    III Multplication        IV. Division
    The CORRECT answer is:
    A. I and II
    B. I and III
    C. II and IV
    D. III and IV
    E. The rules are different for each operation

13. Three of four identical measuring containers  13.____
    are filled as shown at the right. All the
    liquid in the three containers is poured
    into the empty container on the right.
    What fractional part of this container
    will be filled?
    A. 1/10   B. 12/35   C. 7/10   D. 9/10   E. 1

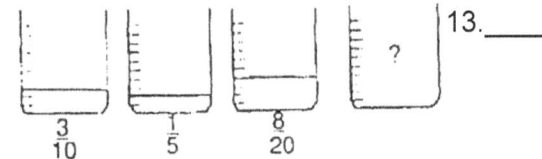

14. 1/2 of 20 is the same as 1/4 of  14.____
    A. 5   B. 10   C. 40   D. 60   E. 80

15. What is the SMALLEST number which can be divided evenly by each of  15.____
    the following numbers: 4, 6, 8?
    A. 48   B. 32   C. 24   D. 16   E. 12

16. (2/3 ÷ 1/2) × $\frac{1}{2}$ =

    A. 1/6   B. 3/8   C. 2/3   D. 3/2   E. 8/3

17. A bank clerk reported that the number of $100 bills in the vault was 10,003. About how much money is this?
    A. $1,000,   B. $10,000   C. $100,000
    D. $1,000,000   E. $10,000,000

18. 3/40 is the same as
    A. .0075   B. .0133   C. .075   D. .1333   E. .75

19.    94/5
    +131 1/4

    A. 22 5/9   B. 22 9/20   C. 23   D. 23 1/20   E. 23 15

20.     36
    52)1872
    To make the answer in the above example four times as large as it is, you could change the number 1872 to
    A. 208   B. 468   C. 936   D. 3944   E. 7488

21. Which of these will produce an even whole number no matter what whole number is put in place of A?
    I. 2 × △ + 1   II. 2 × △ + 2   III. 2 × △ + 3
    The CORRECT answer is:
    A. I only   B. II only   C. III only
    D. I and II only   E. I and III only

22. Which of these shows the CORRECT meaning of 407?
    A. (4 × ten) + (7 × one)
    B. (4 × ten × ten) + (0 × ten) + (7 × one)
    C. (4+0+7) × (one hundred)
    D. (4 × one) + (0 × ten) + (7 × ten × ten)
    E. (4 × one) + (7 × ten)

23. If the scale length of 4 ½ inches represents an actual distance of 72 miles, how many miles does the scale length of 7 inches represent?
    A. 2   B. 56   C. 74 ½   D. 112   E. 504

24. 4 5 6 . 7 2 3 8
    ↑ ↑   ↑ ↑ ↑
    F G   H J K

    In the above numeral, which arrow points to the hundreds place?
    A. F   B. G   C. H   D. J   E. K

25. Which of these is between 5/6 and 7/8?
    A. 2/3   B. 3/4   C. 4/5   D. 6/7   E. 8/9

26. 340.292 ÷ 48.2 =
    A. 706   B. 76   C. 70.6   D. 7.6   E. 7.06

27. Jim started mowing the grass at 1:45 P.M. and finished at 2:15 P.M. How many minutes did Jim take to mow the grass?
    A. 30   B. 70   C. 90   D. 180   E. 240

28. To reduce a fraction to LOWEST terms, what should be done to both numerator and denominator?
    A. Each should be divided by 2.
    B. Each should be multiplied by 2.
    C. Each should be multiplied by the least common multiple.
    D. Each should be divided by the greatest common divisor.
    E. The same number should be subtracted from each.

29. $3 + \sqrt{64} =$
    A. 11   B. 19   C. 24   D. 35   E. $\sqrt{73}$

30. Between 8 A.M. and 3 P.M., the temperature rose 25°. The temperature at 8 A.M. was 10° below zero.
    At 3 P.M., the temperature was _____ zero.
    A. 26° above   B. 15° above   C. 5° above
    D. 5° below    E. 35° below

31. A boy saves 18 dollars in 8 weeks. He continues to save at the same rate. How many weeks will it take him to save 81 dollars?
    A. 13   B. 36   C. 40   D. 71   E. 181 ¼

32. One whole number is divided by another whole number.
    It is ALWAYS TRUE that the
    A. divisor is smaller than the quotient
    B. remainder is smaller than the divisor
    C. quotient is smaller than the divisor
    D. remainder is smaller than the quotient
    E. dividend is smaller than the remainder

33. Which of these will NEVER change the value of a number?
    I. Multiplying it by 1
    II. Dividing it by 1
    III. Multiplying it by its reciprocal
    The CORRECT answer is:
    A. I only           B. II only          C. III only
    D. I and II only    E. I and III only

34. Which of the following equals 7 × (3+9)?
    A. (7×3) + (7×9)  B. (7×9) + (3×9)
    C. (7×3) + (7×9)  D. 7 × 27
    E. 21 + 9

35.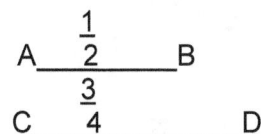

    In the above figure $\dfrac{\text{length of AB}}{\text{length of CD}} =$

    A. 1/2   B. 1/3   C. 2/3   D. 3/2   E. 5/3

36. Which series is NOT in descending order?
    A. 4.04, 4.004, 404   B. 2.1, 1.2, 2.12
    C. .06, .009, .10     D. 13.2, 12/3, 12.03
    E. 736, 631, 367

Questions 37-38.

DIRECTIONS: Questions 37 and 28 are to be answered on the basis of the following graph.

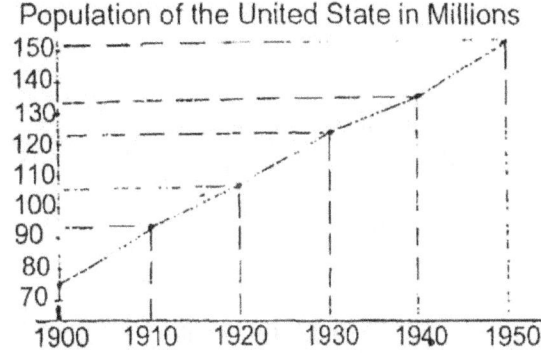

37. According to the above graph, the population of the United States in 1935 was about
    A. 127,000        B. 1,270,000      C. 12,700,000
    D. 127,000,000    E. 1,270,000,000

38. What was the AVERAGE increase per year between 1900 and 1950?
    A. 1,500       B. 15,000      C. 150,000
    D. 750,000     E. 1,500,000

39. What is the radio of 2 gallons to 3 quarts?
    A. 8 to 3   B. 3 to 8   C. 3 to 2   D. 2 to 3   E. 1 to 6

40. What percent of the figure at the right is darkened?
    A. 12
    B. 25
    C. 48
    D. 50
    E. 52

41. A cutting edge .004 inch thick is four times as thick as a second cutting edge. How many inches thick is the second cutting edge?
    A. .001   B. .0032   C. .004   D. .016   E. .04

42. 20% in equal to the fraction $\frac{?}{30}$.
    A. 2/3   B. 6   C. 60   D. 150   E. 600

43. In the figure at the right, the two bars whose lengths have the ratio 2 to 2 are
    A. II and III
    B. IV and I
    C. IV and III
    D. I and III
    E. IV and II

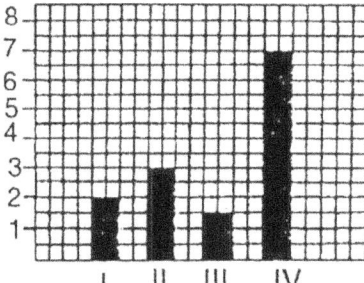

44. The advertisement for a sale reads: *All books reduced more than 20%.* If two books each have the same sale price, which statement MUST be TRUE? The
    A. original prices of both books were the same
    B. original prices of both books were different
    C. percent reduction for both books was the same
    D. sale price of each book is less than 80% of the original price
    E. sale price of each book is more than 80% of the original price.

45. Which of these multiplications will result in an odd number?
    I.  3 0 4 9      II.  7 0 0 2     III.  6 5 4 3    IV.  8 7 6 5
        ×6 4 3 1          ×3 4 8 5          ×3 4 5 6         ×3 4 9 7

    The CORRECT answer is:
    A. I and III only            B. I and IV only
    C. II and IV only            D. II, III, and IV only
    E. All of the above

46. A movie opened in a theatre on April 6 and was shown every day through April 27.
    On how many days was it shown?
    A. 20  B. 21  C. 22
    D. 23  E. None of the above

47. A student has an average of 80 for three tests.
    What must he score on the next test in order to obtain an average of 84?
    A. 80  B. 84  C. 88  D. 91  E. 96

48. Of 28 students in a class, 25 contributed to the Junior Red Cross and 16 to the March of Dimes. Every member of the class contributed to AT LEAST one of the two organizations.
    The number who contributed to both is
    A. 3  B. 12  C. 14  D. 16  E. 25

49. On an arithmetic test, Bill got 32 as an answer to one problem. In working this problem, Bill's only mistake was multiplying by 4 in the last step when he should have divided by 4.
    What is the CORRECT answer to the problem?
    A. 2
    B. 4
    C. 8
    D. 28
    E. It cannot be determined from the information given.

50. Each of two whole numbers is greater than 1. Their product is an odd number. Then, their sum is a(n) _____ their product.
    A. odd number less than
    B. even number less than
    C. odd number greater than
    D. even number greater than
    E. number equal to

## KEY (CORRECT ANSWERS)

| | | | | |
|---|---|---|---|---|
| 1. B | 11. A | 21. B | 31. B | 41. A |
| 2. B | 12. A | 22. B | 32. B | 42. B |
| 3. E | 13. D | 23. D | 33. D | 43. A |
| 4. C | 14. C | 24. A | 34. A | 44. D |
| 5. E | 15. C | 25. D | 35. C | 45. B |
| 6. A | 16. C | 26. E | 36. C | 46. C |
| 7. C | 17. D | 27. A | 37. D | 47. E |
| 8. C | 18. C | 28. D | 38. E | 48. C |
| 9. E | 19. D | 29. A | 39. A | 49. A |
| 10. C | 20. E | 30. B | 40. E | 50. B |

## SOLUTIONS TO PROBLEMS

1. 8 and 7 yield 15 by using sum, since 8 + 7 = 15.

2. To average out a group of numbers, add them and divide by the number of numbers. Ex..
The average of 3, 4, 8 = (3+4+8)/3 = 5.

3. 6428 + 974 + 86 + 7280 + 764 + 5407 = 20,938

4. The inverse of division is multiplication. Ex.: To check that 10 ÷ 2 = 5, we note that (5)(2) = 10.

5. 1 in. to 1 yd. = 1 in. to 36 in. = 1 to 36.

6. 6 is not evenly divisible by 8 since whole number.

7. 5.90 ft. = 5 ft. 10.8 in., which is a reasonable man's height.

8. (2+8) ÷ 2 = 5

9. If P is between X and Y, it corresponds to a point between 8 and 12. It would be impossible for W to be between P and X.

10. The greatest common divisor of 24, 40 and 120 is 8 since 24 ÷ 8, 40 ÷ 8, and 120 ÷ 8 all yield whole numbers. No number larger than 8 will divide evenly into each of 24, 40, and 120.

11. $\frac{2}{3} \neq \frac{4}{9}$ because (2)(9) ≠ (3)(4)

12. For addition and subtraction, the rules for placing the decimal point in the answer are alike, namely, to line up the decimal point for each number.

13. $\frac{3}{10} + \frac{1}{5} + \frac{8}{20} = \frac{3}{10} + \frac{2}{10} + \frac{4}{10} = \frac{9}{10}$

14. Let x = missing number. Then, $(\frac{1}{2})(20) = \frac{1}{4}x$. $10 = \frac{1}{4}$, so x = 40

15. 24 is the smallest number which can divide evenly by 4, 6, and 8. This is called the least common multiple.

16. $(\frac{2}{3} \div \frac{1}{2}) \times \frac{1}{2} = \frac{4}{3} \times \frac{1}{2} = \frac{4}{6} = \frac{2}{3}$

10 (#1)

17. (10,003)($100) = $1000,300 ≈ $1,000,000

18. $\frac{3}{40}$ = .075

19. $9\frac{4}{5} + 13\frac{1}{4} = 9\frac{16}{20} + 13\frac{5}{20} = 22\frac{21}{20} = 23\frac{1}{20}$

20. Using 7488, we get 7488 ÷ 52 = 244, which is 4 times as large as 36.

21. 2x + 2 must be even if x = any whole number. The other choices 2x +1 and 2x + 3 must be odd.

22. 407 = (4 × ten × ten) + (0 × ten) + (7×one).

23. Let x = actual miles. Then, $\frac{4\frac{1}{2}}{72} = \frac{7}{x}$, $4\frac{1}{2}x = 504$, x = 112

24. F points to 4, which is in the hundreds place.

25. lies between and . To check convert to decimals, $.\overline{857142}$ is between $.8\overline{3}$ and .875

26. 340.292 ÷ 48.2 = 7.06

27. From 1:45 PM to 2:15 PM = 30 minutes

28. To completely reduce a fraction, each of numerator and denominator should be divided by the greatest common divisor.

    Ex.: $\frac{18}{30}$ can be reduced to by dividing numerator and denominator by 6. Note: 6 = greatest common divisor of 18 and 30.

29. $3+\sqrt{64}$ = 3+8 = 11

30. -10° + 25° = 15° above zero

31. $81 ÷ $18 = 4.5. Then, (4.5)(8) = 36 weeks

32. When dividing one whole number by another whole number, the remainder must be smaller than the divisor.
    Ex.: 39 ÷ 17 = 2 with a remainder of 5, and 5 < 17.

33. Dividing by 1 or multiplying by 1 will never change the value of a number.

34. 7 × (3+9) = 84 = (7×3)+(7×9)

35. $\frac{1}{2}" ÷ \frac{3}{4}" = (\frac{1}{2})(\frac{4}{3}) = \frac{4}{6} = \frac{2}{3}$

## 11 (#1)

36. .06, .009, 10 is NOT in descending order. The correct order would be .10, .06, .009.

37. In 1935, the population of the U.S. was about 127,000,000.

38. Average increase = (150,000,000 − 75,000,000) ÷ 50 = 1,500,000.

39. 2 gallons = 8 quarts, so 2 gallons : 3 quarts = 8:3

40. There are 13 darkened boxes out of a total of 25 boxes.

    $\frac{13}{25}$ = 52%

41. Second cutting edge = .004" ÷ 4 = .001 in.

42. $20\% = \frac{1}{5} = \frac{6}{30}$

43. Bar II = 3 units, bar III = 1 ½ units, and 3 to 1 ½ = 2 to 1.

44. If a price is reduced by more than 20%, the sales price MUST be less than 80% of the original price. Ex: Original price = $100, reduced by 22%, sales price = $78 = 78% of original price.

45. Since 9×1 = odd and 5×7 = odd, both (3049)(6431) and (8765)(3497) must result in an odd number.

46. 27 − 6 + 1 + 22 days.

47. Let x = score on 4$^{th}$ test. Then, (80)(3) + x = (84)(4). 240 ÷ x = 336. Solving, x = 96

48. Let x = number who contributed to both, 25 − x = number who contributed only to Junior Red Cross, 16 − x = number who contributed only to March of Dimes. Then, x + 25-x+16 −x = 28, so x =13.

49. Since he multiplied by 4, the next to last number = 8. So, 8 ÷ 4 = 2.

50. Since their product is odd, each number must be odd. Their sum is an even number les than their product.
    Ex: 3 + 5 = 8 < (3)(5) = 15

# EXAMINATION SECTION
## TEST 1

DIRECTIONS: Each question or incomplete statement is followed by several suggested answers or completions. Select the one that BEST answers the question or completes the statement. *PRINT THE LETTER OF THE CORRECT ANSWER IN THE SPACE AT THE RIGHT.*

1. 6.030 - 5.008 =

    A. 1.922   B. 1.092   C. .922   D. 1.022

    1._____

2. $\frac{3}{8} \times \frac{2}{3} =$

    A. $1\frac{1}{4}$   B. $\frac{5}{8}$   C. $\frac{1}{3}$   D. $\frac{1}{4}$

    2._____

3. $2 \times 3\frac{3}{4} =$

    A. $7\frac{3}{4}$   B. $6\frac{3}{4}$   C. $7\frac{1}{2}$   D. $6\frac{1}{2}$

    3._____

4. $\frac{1}{6} + \frac{1}{4} + \frac{1}{2} =$

    A. $\frac{11}{12}$   B. $\frac{7}{6}$   C. $\frac{3}{12}$   D. 1

    4._____

5. If 367 + 26 = 373 + n, n =

    A. 0   B. 2   C. 6   D. 20

    5._____

6. $\frac{5}{8} \div 4 =$

    A. $2\frac{1}{2}$   B. $1\frac{1}{8}$   C. $\frac{5}{32}$   D. $\frac{1}{8}$

    6._____

7. 3 hours 5 minutes
   -2 hours 55 minutes

    A. 1 hr. 10 min.   B. 1 hr. 5 min.
    C. 50 min.         D. 10 min.

    7._____

8. If $\frac{3}{8} = \frac{n}{24}$, n =

   A. 16    B. 9    C. 5    D. 3

9. If 336 ÷ 8 = 40 + n, n =

   A. 4 1/2    B. 2    C. 3/4    D. 0

10. What is the sum of 2 feet 2 inches and 1 foot 6 inches?

    A. 1 yd. 2'8"    B. 1 yd. 1'8"
    C. 1 yd. 8"      D. 3 yd. 8"

11. 30% of 30 =

    A. 9.0    B. 0.9    C. 90.0    D. 60.0

12. $\frac{1}{6} - \frac{1}{7} =$

    A. 1/42    B. 1/13
    C. 1       D. none of the above

13. If 5/8 = 45/n, n =

    A. 40    B. 48    C. 64    D. 72

14. What is 1 yard 4 inches divided by 2?

    A. 10"    B. 1'2"    C. 1'8"    D. 1'10"

15. 1 foot 6 inches is what percent of one yard?

    A. 40    B. 50    C. 60    D. 200

16. If the scale on a road map is *twelve miles to one inch,* a road 112 miles long would be represented by a line

    A. 12"    B. 11 1/5"    C. 10"    D. 9 1/4"

17. During a sale a $25 toaster was reduced 15%. What was the sale price?

    A. $24.50    B. $21.25    C. $22.50    D. $20.00

18. 89 is 89% of

    A. 189    B. 100    C. 89    D. 1

19. If a man has a step which averages 32 inches, how many steps would he take to cover 16 feet?

    A. 2    B. 5    C. 6    D. 20

20. Sum is to difference as product is to

    A. subtrahend    B. multiplicand
    C. divisor       D. quotient

21. Which of the following has the GREATEST value?

    A. 3% of 600    B. 2% of 800    C. 4% of 400    D. 5% of 200

22. 8.3% is equivalent to

    A. .0083    B. .083    C. .83    D. 8.3

23. What number must be put in the △'s to make (3x△) - (2+△) equal 14?

    A. 8    B. 7    C. 6    D. 3

24. The number nine thousand twenty and sixteen thousandths can be written

    A. 9020.160    B. 9020.016    C. 9020.0016    D. 920.016

25. If a plane that uses 40 gallons of gasoline per hour is to take a 6-hour trip and carry 10% extra gasoline for safety, how many gallons of gasoline should be put in the plane?

    A. 244    B. 246    C. 240.6    D. 264

26. If 103 x 200 = 600 + n, n =

    A. (100x200)    B. (103x100)    C. (3x600)    D. (10x200)

27. What number must be put in the n to make $6 \times \frac{7}{\square}$ equal 14?

    A. 7    B. 6    C. 3    D. 2

Questions 28-30.

DIRECTIONS: Questions 28 through 30 are to be answered on the basis of the following graph.

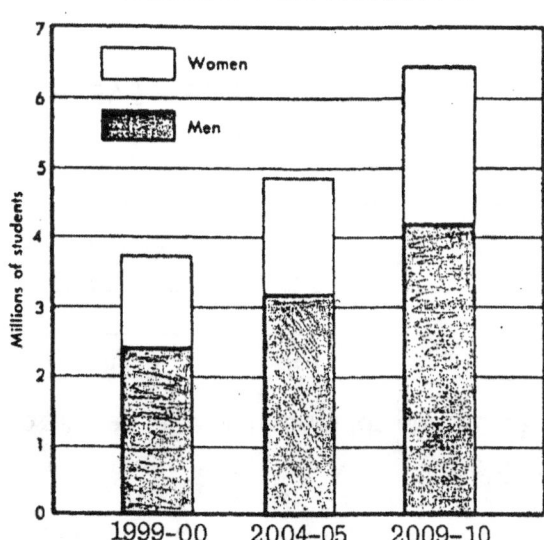

1999 PROJECTIONS OF REGULAR SESSION COLLEGE ENROLLMENT FOR THE 2000'S

4 (#1)

28. The increase in the number of men students from 2004-05 to 2009-2010 is expected to be about    28._____

   A. 10,000,000  B. 5,000,000
   C. 1,000,000   D. 500,000

29. Which of the following would be the BEST estimate of the number of men that will be in college in 2007-08?    29._____

   A. 5,600,000  B. 5,000,000
   C. 4,100,000  D. 3,700,000

30. It is predicted that the number of college women in 2009-10 will be APPROXIMATELY    30._____

   A. 220,000   B. 640,000   C. 2,200,000   D. 6,400,000

31. Which of the following is of greatest value?    31._____

   A. 11/16   B. .812   C. 5/8   D. .789

32. If a particular type of mail advertisement brings 20% response, how many copies of the advertisement should be sent to get 500 responses?    32._____

   A. 500   B. 2500   C. 1000   D. 5000

33. In one town tomatoes are selling at 3 pounds for 72 cents. At this rate, how much would you pay for 3 1/2 pounds?    33._____

   A. $1.32   B. $1.08   C. $0.96   D. $0.84

34. If a ridge in a piece of machinery is to have a length of 27/100 inch plus or minus 8/1000 inch, an inspector would accept a ridge with a length of    34._____

   A. 20/100"   B. 29/100"   C. 263/1000"   D. 301/1000"

Questions 35-37.

DIRECTIONS: Questions 35 through 37 are to be answered on the basis of the following table.

SHOOTING RECORD OF THE MEMBERS OF A BASKETBALL TEAM

| Player | Shots Attempted | Shots Made |
| --- | --- | --- |
| Jones | 27 | 11 |
| Smith | 5 | 0 |
| Allen | 18 | 8 |
| Lyons | 11 | 5 |
| Olson | 14 | 2 |

35. The five players as a team made approximately what percent of their shots?    35._____

   A. 20   B. 25   C. 30   D. 35

36. Which player has the highest ratio of number of shots made to number of shots attempted?    36._____

   A. Lyons   B. Allen   C. Jones   D. Olson

37. If Allen had taken as many shots as Jones and maintained his shooting rate, how many shots would he have made?

   A. 13　　　B. 12　　　C. 11　　　D. 10

37.____

38. If each ring of a telephone bell is 1.1 seconds long with .6 second between rings, the time from the beginning of the first ring to the end of the sixth ring would be _____ sec.

   A. 6.6　　　B. 9.6　　　C. 13.2　　　D. 10.2

38.____

39. $\sqrt{.04} =$

   A. .2　　　B. .02　　　C. .002　　　D. 2.00

39.____

40. $3^2 =$

   A. $\sqrt{81}$　　　B. $2^3$　　　C. $\sqrt{3}$　　　D. $\sqrt[3]{2}$

40.____

Questions 41-43.

DIRECTIONS: Questions 41 through 43 are to be answered on the basis of the following values.

　　h represents the value of one chair

　　↑ represents the value of one umbrella

　　╫ represents the value of one belt

The value of a chair h is 12 times the value of an umbrella ↑, and the value of an umbrella is five times the value of a belt ╫.

　　h = 12 ↑　　　　↑ = 5 ╫

41. 2 ↑ - 3 ╫ =

   A. ↑ + ╫　　　B. ↑ + 2 ╫　　　C. 6 ╫　　　D. 2 ╫

41.____

42. The difference between 2 h + 3 ╫ and h + ↑ + 4 ╫ is

   A. h + 11 ↑ + ╫　　B. h - ╫　　C. 10 ↑ + 4 ╫　　D. 9 ╫

42.____

43. 15 ╫ =

   A. 1/3 ↑　　　B. 4 ↑　　　C. 1/4 h　　　D. h

43.____

44. The number 40, base ten, would be written 1111 in base

   A. three　　　B. two　　　C. four　　　D. twelve

44.____

45. If we write all numbers in base eight notation, $24_{eight} + 15_{eight} + 12_{eight} =$

   A. $51_{eight}$　　　B. $52_{eight}$　　　C. $54_{eight}$　　　D. $53_{eight}$

45.____

## KEY (CORRECT ANSWERS)

| | | | | |
|---|---|---|---|---|
| 1. D | 11. A | 21. A | 31. B | 41. B |
| 2. D | 12. A | 22. B | 32. B | 42. C |
| 3. C | 13. D | 23. A | 33. D | 43. C |
| 4. A | 14. C | 24. B | 34. C | 44. A |
| 5. D | 15. B | 25. D | 35. D | 45. A |
| 6. C | 16. D | 26. A | 36. A | |
| 7. D | 17. B | 27. C | 37. B | |
| 8. B | 18. B | 28. C | 38. B | |
| 9. B | 19. C | 29. D | 39. A | |
| 10. C | 20. D | 30. C | 40. A | |

# SOLUTIONS TO PROBLEMS

1. $6.030 - 5.008 = 1.022$

2. $\dfrac{3}{8} \times \dfrac{2}{3} = \dfrac{6}{24} = \dfrac{1}{4}$

3. $2 \times 3\dfrac{3}{4} = \dfrac{2}{1} \times \dfrac{15}{4} = \dfrac{30}{4} = 7\dfrac{1}{2}$

4. $\dfrac{1}{6} + \dfrac{1}{4} + \dfrac{1}{2} = \dfrac{2}{12} + \dfrac{3}{12} + \dfrac{6}{12} = \dfrac{11}{12}$

5. $367 + 26 = 373 + n$, $n = 367 + 26 - 373 = 20$

6. $\dfrac{5}{8} \div 4 = \dfrac{5}{8} \times \dfrac{1}{4} = \dfrac{5}{32}$

7. 3 hrs. 5 min. - 2 hrs. 55 min. = 2 hrs. 65 min. - 2 hrs. 55 min. = 10 min.

8. $\dfrac{3}{8} = \dfrac{n}{24}$, $8n = 72$, $n = 9$

9. $336 \div 8 = 40 + n$, $42 = 40 + n$, $n = 2$

10. 2 ft. 2 in. + 1 ft. 6 in. = 3 ft. 8 in. = 1 yd. 8 in.

11. 30% of 30 = .30 x 30 = 9

12. $\dfrac{1}{6} - \dfrac{1}{7} = \dfrac{7}{42} - \dfrac{6}{42} = \dfrac{1}{42}$

13. $\dfrac{5}{8} = \dfrac{45}{n}$, $5n = 360$, $n = 72$

14. (1 yd. 4 in.) ÷ 2 = 40 in. ÷ 2 = 20 in. = 1 ft. 8 in.

15. 1 ft. 6 in. ÷ 1 yd. = 18 in. ÷ 36 in. = 1/2 = 50%

16. 112 ÷ 12 = 9 1/3 in.

17. Sale price = ($25)(.85) = $21.25

8 (#1)

18. 89 = 89% of x, x = 89 ÷ .89 = 100

19. 16 ft. ÷ 32 in. = 192 in. ÷ 32 in. = 6 steps

20. Sum : Difference = Product : Quotient

21. 3% of 600 = 18, 2% of 800 = 16, 4% of 400 = 16,
    5% of 200 = 10. 3% of 600 is highest.

22. 8.3% = .083

23. 3 x △ - (2+ △ ) = 2 x △ - 2 = 14.  △ = (14+2)/2 = 8

24. Nine thousand twenty and sixteen thousandths = 9020.016

25. (40)(6) + (.10)(40)(6) = 264 gallons

26. 103 x 200 = 600 + n; 20,600= 600 + n; n = 20,000 = 100 x 200

27. $6 \times \dfrac{7}{\square} = 14$, $\dfrac{7}{\square} = \dfrac{14}{6}$, $14 \times \square = 42$, $\square = 3$

28. Increase ≈ 4.25 million - 3.25 million = 1,000,000

29. Roughly halfway between 3.25 million and 4.25 million ≈ 3,700,000

30. 6.5 million - 4.25 million = 2.25 million ≈ 2,200,000

31. 11/16 = .6875 and 5/8 = .625, so selection B (.812) has the largest value of the given selections.

32. Let x = number of copies sent. Then 500 = .20x, x = 2500

33. .72 ÷ 3 = .24 per pound. Then, (.24)(3 1/2) = .84

34. $\dfrac{27}{100} \pm \dfrac{8}{1000} = \dfrac{262}{1000}$ to $\dfrac{278}{1000}$. So, $\dfrac{263}{1000}$ is acceptable.

35. (11+0+8+5+2)/(27+5+18+11+14) = 26/75 ≈ 35%

36. Lyons: 5/11 = 45.$\overline{45}$%; Allen: 8/18 = 44.$\overline{4}$%; Jones: 11/27 = 40.$\overline{740}$%;

    Olson: 2/14 ≈ 14.3%. Lyons has the highest ratio.

37. Allen's ratio = 44.$\overline{4}$%. Then, (.$\overline{4}$)(27) = 12 shots made.

38. Total time = (6)(1.1) + (5)(.6) = 9.6 sec.

9 (#1)

39. $\sqrt{.04} = .2$

40. $3^2 = (3)(3) = 9 = \sqrt{81}$

41. 2↑ - 3✝ - = 10✝ - 3✝ = 7✝ = ↑ + 2✝

42. (2⋂ + 3✝) - (⋂ + ↑ + 4✝) = ⋂ - ↑ - ✝ = 54✝ = 10↑ + 4✝

43. 15✝ = 3↑ = 1/4 ⋂

44. $1111_{\text{base 3}} = (1)(3^3) + (1)(3^2) + (1)(3^1) + (1)(3^0) =$

    $27 + 9 + 3 + 1 = 40_{\text{base 10}}$

45. $24_{\text{eight}} + 15_{\text{eight}} + 12_{\text{eight}} = 51_{\text{eight}} = (5)(8) + (1)(8^0) = 43_{\text{ten}}$

---

# QUANTITATIVE COMPARISONS

# EXAMINATION SECTION
# TEST 1

DIRECTIONS: Each of the following questions has two parts. One is in Column A. The other part is in Column B. You must find out if one part is greater than the other, or if the parts are equal.
Mark the answer:
   A if the part in Column A is greater,
   B if the part in Column B is greater,
   C if the two parts are equal.
*PRINT THE LETTER OF THE CORRECT ANSWER IN THE SPACE AT THE RIGHT.*

| COLUMN A | COLUMN B | |
|---|---|---|
| 1. 2 + 3 | 4 + 1 | 1.____ |
| 2. 1 dozen | 10 | 2.____ |
| 3. Number of dots (15) | Number of dots (16) | 3.____ |
| 4. Area of the shaded region | One-half the area of the circle | 4.____ |
| 5. Time: 60 minutes | Time: 60 seconds | 5.____ |
| 6. Speed as shown above | Speed as shown above | 6.____ |

105

2 (#1)

| COLUMN A | COLUMN B | |
|---|---|---|
| 7. 27<br>×3 | 27<br>27<br>27<br>+27 | 7.____ |
| 8. This morning<br><br>Minutes <u>before</u> noon today on this clock | This afternoon<br><br>Minutes <u>after</u> noon today on this clock | 8.____ |
| 9. One-tenth | $\frac{1}{10}$ | 9.____ |
| 10. 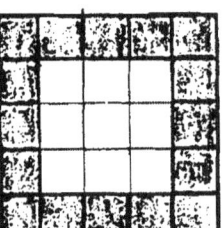<br>Number of white squares | Number of dark squares | 10.____ |
| 11. $0.90 | 3 × $0.03 | 11.____ |

Questions 12-13.

DIRECTIONS: Questions 12 through 13 are to be answered on the basis of the following table.

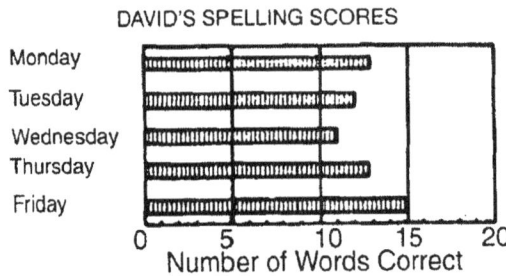

| 12. David's score on Monday | His score on Friday | 12.____ |
|---|---|---|
| 13. His average score for Thursday and Friday | His average score for Tuesday and Wednesday | 13.____ |

3 (#1)

| COLUMN A | COLUMN B | |
|---|---|---|
| 14. (5 x 60) - (4 x 60) | (7 x 60) - (5 x 60) | 14.____ |

15.                                                                                                               15.____

```
0  1  2           7  8  9  10
|__|__|__|__|__|__|__|__|__|
```

The number of <u>even</u> numbers that are not named on this segment of the number line.

The number of <u>odd</u> numbers that are not named on this segment of the number line.

16.                                                                                                               16.____

 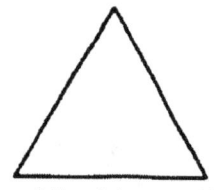

Distance around the square if each side has length 3

Distance around the triangle if each side has length 4

17.  $\frac{1}{3}+\frac{1}{4}$              $\frac{1}{12}$                                                        17.____

18.  378 + 381                              379 + 380                                                             18.____

19.  Number of eighths equal to 1/4        Number of sixths equal to $\frac{1}{3}$                                19.____

20.  Number of days in 6 weeks, not counting Sundays    Number of days in 7 weeks, not counting Saturdays and Sundays    20.____

21.                                                                                                               21.____

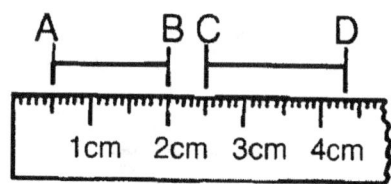

Length of AB                               Length of CD

22.              100 centimeters = 1 meter                                                                        22.____
     Length of 0.2 meter                   Length of 20 centimeters

107

COLUMN A　　　　　　　　　　　COLUMN B

23. $300 + \square + 6 = 346$　　　　$\triangle + 40 + 6 = 346$　　　　　23.____

　　　The number that goes in $\square$　　The number that goes in $\triangle$

24. Speed at 1 kilometer per minutes　　Speed at 60 kilometers per hour　　24.____

25. $\dfrac{1+1+1}{3}$　　　　　　　　$\dfrac{1+1+1+1}{4}$　　　　　　25.____

## KEY (CORRECT ANSWERS)

1. C　　　11. A
2. A　　　12. B
3. B　　　13. A
4. B　　　14. B
5. A　　　15. C

6. A　　　16. C
7. B　　　17. A
8. B　　　18. C
9. C　　　19. C
10. B　　　20. A

21. B
22. C
23. B
24. C
25. C

# TEST 2

DIRECTIONS: Each of the following questions has two parts. One is in Column A. The other part is in Column B. You must find out if one part is greater than the other, or if the parts are equal.
Mark the answer:
   A if the part in Column A is greater,
   B if the part in Column B is greater,
   C if the two parts are equal.
*PRINT THE LETTER OF THE CORRECT ANSWER IN THE SPACE AT THE RIGHT.*

| COLUMN A | COLUMN B | |
|---|---|---|
| 1. The sum: 3+5 plus any whole number greater than 1 | The sum: 3 + 5 + 1 | 1.____ |
| 2. The next <u>whole</u> number after 6 | The next <u>even</u> number after 6 | 2.____ |
| 3. | | 3.____ |

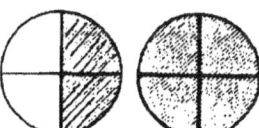

Each of the four equal circles is divided into four equal parts.

| | | |
|---|---|---|
| Sum of shaded parts in A and B | Sum of shaded parts in C and D | 3.____ |
| 4. 3)63̄ | 2)42̄ | 4.____ |
| 5. | | 5.____ |

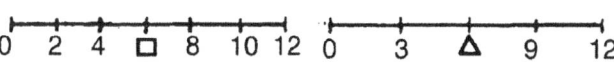

| | | |
|---|---|---|
| The number □ on this number line | The number △ on this number line | 5.____ |
| 6. 400 minus 110 | 400 minus 120 | 6.____ |
| 7. $\frac{1}{2} + \frac{1}{2}$ | $\frac{1}{3} + \frac{2}{3}$ | 7.____ |
| 8. Some number between 2 and 6 | Some number between 7 and 11 | 8.____ |
| 9. The number of tens in 38 | The number of hundreds in 438 | 9.____ |

2 (#2)

| | COLUMN A | COLUMN B | |
|---|---|---|---|
| 10. | Amount of milk in 1,000 liters of milk | Amount of milk in 1 kiloliter of milk | 10._____ |
| 11. | $1.11 | Value of 11 dimes | 11._____ |
| 12. | 9,634 ×6,825 | 6,825 ×9,634 | 12._____ |
| 13. | 3 x (1+1+1+1+1) | 5 x (1+1+1) | 13._____ |
| 14. | Number of years since you were 2 years old | Number of years since you were 4 years old | 14._____ |
| 15. | 3 x 9 x 2 | 3 x 3 x 5 | 15._____ |
| 16. | Weight of 100 grams | 100 centigrams = 1 gram Weight of 1 centigram | 16._____ 16._____ |
| 17. | $\frac{1}{5}$ | $\frac{1}{4}$ | 17._____ |
| 18. | $4.00 | Cost of 4 boxes of candy at $0.99 per box | 18._____ |
| 19. | The number ☐ if ☐ + 3 = 5 | The number △ if △ -2=2 | 19._____ |
| 20. | 64 ÷ 8 | 63 ÷ 9 | 20._____ |
| 21. | Number of dimes equal to $0.50 | Number of nickels equal to $0.25 | 21._____ |
| 22. | 8 + 8 | ̶H̶H̶ ||| + ̶H̶H̶ ||| | 22._____ |
| 23. | Total number of apples in 3 baskets of 9 apples each | Total number of apples in 4 baskets of 7 apples each | 23._____ |
| 24. | 0 | 0 x 2 | 24._____ |
| 25. | 10,000 | 100 x 100 | 25._____ |

# KEY (CORRECT ANSWERS)

1. A
2. B
3. A
4. C
5. C

6. A
7. C
8. B
9. B
10. C

11. A
12. C
13. C
14. A
15. A

16. A
17. B
18. A
19. B
20. A

21. C
22. C
23. B
24. C
25. C

---

# TEST 3

DIRECTIONS: Each of the following questions has two parts. One part is in Column A. The other part is in Column B. You must find out if one part is greater than the other, or if the parts are equal, or if not enough information is given for you to decide.

Mark the answer:
- A if the part in Column A is greater,
- B if the part in Column B is greater,
- C if the two parts are equal,
- D if not enough information is given for you to decide.

Note: Letters such as x, n, and k stand for real numbers. If the same letter appears in both columns of a question, it stands for the same number.

*PRINT THE LETTER OF THE CORRECT ANSWER IN THE SPACE AT THE RIGHT.*

| | COLUMN A | COLUMN B | |
|---|---|---|---|
| 1. | 2 + 8 | 13-2 | 1.____ |
| 2. | 10 | Number of centimeters in 1 meter | 2.____ |
| 3. | 2.5 | 5.2 | 3.____ |
| 4. | The amount of money Jim has if he has 4 coins | The amount of money Bill has if he has 7 coins | 4.____ |
| 5. | Amount of money in one quarter, one dime, and one nickel | $0.35 | 5.____ |
| 6. | (350x860) + (350x1) | (350x861) | 6.____ |
| 7. | Length of AB | Length of CD | 7.____ |
| 8. | (2 x 6) + 3 | (15 x 2) - 15 | 8.____ |
| 9. | 50% | $\dfrac{49}{100}$ | 9.____ |
| 10. | 467 | 4 + (6x10) + (7x100) | 10.____ |
| 11. | Area of this rectangle (3cm × 4cm) | Area of this rectangle (2cm × 6cm) | 11.____ |

For question 7: segment from A with length 8 to a point, then 2 more to C, with B between (AB = 8), and CD = 6 (from just before C to D).

112

2 (#3)

| | COLUMN A | COLUMN B | |
|---|---|---|---|
| 12. | 13 + 15 + 16 + 18 | 14 + 15 + 16 + 17 | 12.____ |
| 13. | Distance traveled in 1/2 hour at 70 kilometers per hour | Distance traveled in 1/3 hour at 105 kilometers per hour | 13.____ |
| 14. | Mrs. Stein's weight, if she weighs twice as much as her daughter | Mrs. Barnum's weight if she weighs three times as much as her daughter | 14.____ |
| 15. | (6 x 8) + (3 x 8) | 72 | 15.____ |
| 16. | $\dfrac{2 \times 3 \times 5 \times 7}{10}$ | $\dfrac{2 \times 3 \times 5 \times 7}{14}$ | 16.____ |
| 17. | The number of <u>even</u> numbers greater than 2 but less than 9 | The number of <u>odd</u> numbers greater than 2 but less than 9 | 17.____ |
| 18. | z if (2 x z) - 6 = 0 | y if (3 x y) - 9 = 0 | 18.____ |
| 19. | 0.472 | $\dfrac{400}{1,000} + \dfrac{70}{1,000} + \dfrac{2}{1,000}$ | 19.____ |
| 20. | The number of days in a year | 356 days | 20.____ |
| 21. | x if 9 + x = 21 | y if 9 + y = 11 | 21.____ |
| 22. | Number of integers between -10 and +10 | Number of integers between -20 and +20 | 22.____ |
| 23. | 3 x 25 | $\dfrac{3 \times 100}{4}$ | 23.____ |

24.   1 rallod = 10 paldas   24.____
      1 palda = 5 kanigs

The value in rallods of 30 paldas and 10 kanigs

The value in rallods of 50 paldas and 5 kanigs

25.   25.____

25% of the liquid in the container

50% of the liquid in this container

## KEY (CORRECT ANSWERS)

1. B
2. B
3. B
4. D
5. A

6. C
7. A
8. C
9. A
10. B

11. C
12. C
13. C
14. D
15. C

16. A
17. C
18. C
19. C
20. A

21. A
22. B
23. C
24. B
25. D

# TEST 4

DIRECTIONS: Each of the following questions has two parts. One part is in Column A. The other part is in Column B. You must find out if one part is greater than the other, or if the parts are equal, or if not enough information is given for you to decide.
Mark the answer:
   A if the part in Column A is greater,
   B if the part in Column B is greater,
   C if the two parts are equal,
   D if not enough information is given for you to decide.
Note: Letters such as x, n, and k stand for real numbers. If the same letter appears in both columns of a question, it stands for the same number.
*PRINT THE LETTER OF THE CORRECT ANSWER IN THE SPACE AT THE RIGHT.*

| | COLUMN A | COLUMN B | |
|---|---|---|---|
| 1. | $\dfrac{473}{31}$ | $\dfrac{473}{3.1}$ | 1.____ |
| 2. | 0  1          5<br>Sum of the missing whole numbers on the part of the number line above | 6  7    9  10<br>The missing whole number on the part of the number line above | 2.____ |
| 3. | $\dfrac{6}{7} \times \dfrac{7}{6}$ | $\dfrac{3}{5} \times \dfrac{5}{3}$ | 3.____ |
| 4. | $\begin{array}{r} 2 \\ 9 \\ +3 \\ \hline \end{array}$ | x is a whole number<br>$\begin{array}{r} 4 \\ 7 \\ +x \\ \hline \end{array}$ | 4.____ |
| 5. | $\dfrac{9}{30}$ | 33 1/3 % | 5.____ |
| 6. | $\dfrac{1}{3} + \dfrac{1}{3} + \dfrac{1}{3}$ | $\dfrac{1}{4} + \dfrac{1}{4} + \dfrac{1}{4} + \dfrac{1}{4}$ | 6.____ |
| 7. | 1.00073 | 1.0063 | 7.____ |

2 (#4)

| COLUMN A | COLUMN B | |
|---|---|---|
| 8. 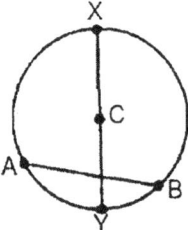 Length of segment XY | Length of segment AB | 8.____ |
| 9. A whole number that is greater than 3 | A whole number that is less than 8 | 9.____ |

Questions 10-13.

DIRECTIONS: Questions 10 through 13 are to be answered on the basis of the circle graph below which gives information about the distribution of the world population.

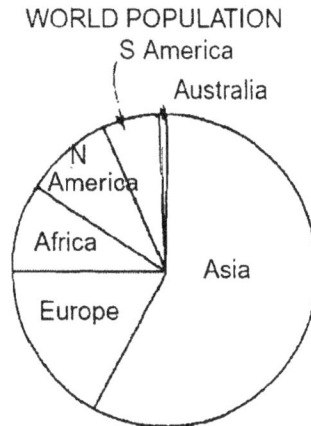

| | | |
|---|---|---|
| 10. Population of South America | Population of Australia | 10.____ |
| 11. Population of Asia | Population of the world, not counting Asia | 11.____ |
| 12. 50% of the world population | Population of Asia | 12.____ |
| 13. Population of Australia | Population of Pakistan | 13.____ |
| 14. $\begin{array}{r}32\\\times 20\end{array}$ | $\begin{array}{r}20\\\times 30\end{array}$ | 14.____ |
| 15. $\dfrac{9}{8} \div \dfrac{3}{8}$ | 3 | 15.____ |
| 16. One million | 1,000 × 100 | 16.____ |

116

|     | COLUMN A | COLUMN B |     |
|-----|----------|----------|-----|

17. The average of 15 and 45 — The average of 15, 30, and 45 — 17.____

18. An area of 1 square meter — Area of rectangle 150 centimeters long and 50 centimeters wide — 18.____

19. Distance represented by 0.5 centimeter on a map with scale: 1 centimeter represents 8 kilometers — Distance represented by 2 centimeters on a map with scale: 1 centimeter represents 4 kilometers — 19.____

20. $\dfrac{3}{x}$ — *x is greater than zero* — $3x$ — 20.____

21. *r, s, and t are consecutive whole numbers listed in increasing order*
    $r + 3$ — $t + 1$ — 21.____

22. $\dfrac{1+0}{1+1-0}$ — $\dfrac{0+1}{1+1-1}$ — 22.____

23. 3% of the cost of 5 books — 5% of the cost of 3 books — 23.____

24. The number obtained by rounding 7,372 to the nearest 1,000 — 7,000 — 24.____

25. *Angle p is greater than angle q.*
    Height of tree A — Height of tree B — 25.____

(Diagram: two trees at points A and B, each 15m from a point between them; angles p and q formed at that point looking up to the tops of trees A and B respectively.)

3 (#4)

117

## KEY (CORRECT ANSWERS)

| | | | |
|---|---|---|---|
| 1. | B | 11. | A |
| 2. | A | 12. | B |
| 3. | C | 13. | D |
| 4. | D | 14. | A |
| 5. | B | 15. | C |
| 6. | C | 16. | A |
| 7. | B | 17. | C |
| 8. | A | 18. | A |
| 9. | D | 19. | B |
| 10. | A | 20. | D |

21. C
22. B
23. D
24. C
25. A

# TEST 5

DIRECTIONS: Each of the following questions has two parts. One part is in Column A. The other part is in Column B. You must find out if one part is greater than the other, or if the parts are equal, or if not enough information is given for you to decide.

Mark your answer:
- A if the part in Column A is greater,
- B if the part in Column B is greater,
- C if the two parts are equal,
- D if not enough information is given for you to decide.

Note: Letters such as x, n, and k stand for real numbers. If the same letter appears in both columns of a question, it stands for the same number.

*PRINT THE LETTER OF THE CORRECT ANSWER IN THE SPACE AT THE RIGHT.*

| COLUMN A | COLUMN B | |
|---|---|---|
| 1. 100% | $\dfrac{16}{17}$ | 1.____ |
| 2. 6 x 6 x 2 | 12 x 12 | 2.____ |
| 3. Length of AB | Segments AC and BD have equal lengths. Length of CD | 3.____ |

(Points A, B, C, D on a line)

| | | |
|---|---|---|
| 4. Z x Z | Z is a number greater than zero. 2 x Z x Z | 4.____ |
| 5. 0.600 + 0.080 + 0.003 | 0.600 + 0.030 + 0.008 | 5.____ |
| 6. Area of shaded portion of figure | Two circle with center O 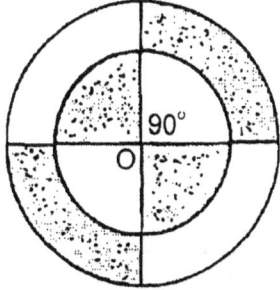 Area of unshaded portion of figure | 6.____ |
| 7. x | $\dfrac{2}{3} = \dfrac{4}{x}$  5 | 7.____ |

2 (#5)

| COLUMN A | COLUMN B | |
|---|---|---|
| 8. Number of days in month X | Number of days in 4 weeks | 8.____ |
| 9. x if 0.2x = 5 | x if 0.2x = 5 | 9.____ |
| 10. $\dfrac{4+6+8}{3}$ | $\dfrac{2+4+6+8+10}{5}$ | 10.____ |
| 11. $1 \div 2$ | $2 \div 1$ | 11.____ |
| 12. $100,000 \div 1,000$ | $100,000 \div 100$ | 12.____ |
| 13. $\dfrac{1}{3}, \dfrac{1}{8}, \dfrac{1}{4}$ <br> The greatest fraction above | $\dfrac{1}{7}, \dfrac{1}{5}, \dfrac{1}{2}$ <br> The greatest fraction above | 13.____ |

14. x, y, and z are consecutive whole numbers in increasing order

| $\dfrac{x+z}{2}$ | y | 14.____ |
|---|---|---|

15. x and y are positive numbers
    x - y = 3

| x | 3 | 15.____ |
|---|---|---|

| 16. Three times the diameter of circle A | Circumference of circle A | 16.____ |
|---|---|---|
| 17. $\dfrac{60}{80} = \dfrac{x}{100}$ <br> x | $\dfrac{3}{4} = y\%$ <br> y | 17.____ |
| 18. 5/0.1 | 5 | 18.____ |

19.

AD is a straight line

| x | y | 19.____ |
|---|---|---|

| 20. (30x575) - (29x575) | (40x575) - (39x575) | 20.____ |
|---|---|---|
| 21. x + 2 | 2x | 21.____ |

| COLUMN A | COLUMN B |

Questions 22-25.

DIRECTIONS: Questions 22 through 25 are to be answered on the basis of the following graph.

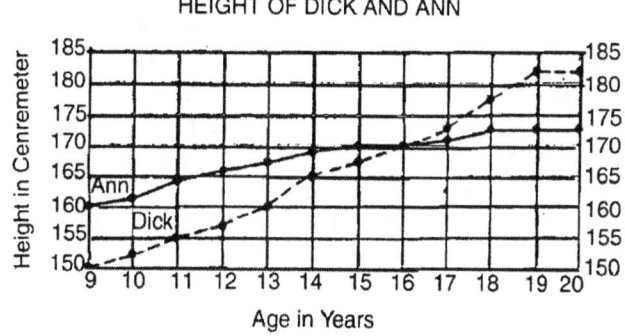

HEIGHT OF DICK AND ANN

| | | |
|---|---|---|
| 22. | The height of Dick at 18 years of age | The height of Ann at 18 years of age | 22.____ |
| 23. | The height of Ann at 16 years of age | The height of Dick at 16 years of age | 23.____ |
| 24. | Ann's age when she was taller than Dick | Dick's age when he was taller than Ann | 24.____ |
| 25. | Difference between Ann's and Dick's ages when Dick was 16 years of age | Difference between Ann's and Dick's ages in 1956 | 25.____ |

# KEY (CORRECT ANSWERS)

| | | | |
|---|---|---|---|
| 1. | A | 11. | B |
| 2. | B | 12. | B |
| 3. | C | 13. | B |
| 4. | B | 14. | C |
| 5. | A | 15. | A |
| 6. | D | 16. | B |
| 7. | A | 17. | C |
| 8. | D | 18. | A |
| 9. | B | 19. | B |
| 10. | C | 20. | C |

21. D
22. A
23. C
24. B
25. D

# TEST 6

DIRECTIONS: Each of the following questions has two parts. One part is in Column A. The other part is in Column B. You must find out if one part is greater than the other, or if the parts are equal, or if not enough information is given for you to decide.
Mark your answer:
   A if the part in Column A is greater,
   B if the part in Column B is greater,
   C if the two parts are equal,
   D if not enough information is given for you to decide.
Note: Letters such as x, n, and k stand for real numbers. If the same letter appears in both columns of a question, it stands for the same number.
*PRINT THE LETTER OF THE CORRECT ANSWER IN THE SPACE AT THE RIGHT.*

| | COLUMN A | COLUMN B | |
|---|---|---|---|
| 1. | $\frac{1}{8}$ of 8 | $\frac{1}{9}$ of 9 | 1.____ |
| 2. | Length L | area 64, W, L; L + W = 16; Length W | 2.____ |
| 3. | $3^3$ | 3×3 | 3.____ |
| 4. | 2x + y | x = 1, y = 2; 2y + x | 4.____ |
| 5. | N | N > 6; 8 | 5.____ |
| 6. | $\frac{2}{3} + \frac{3}{4}$ | $\frac{5}{12}$ | 6.____ |
| 7. | x | 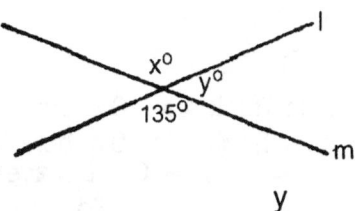 y | 7.____ |

123

2 (#6)

| COLUMN A | COLUMN B | |
|---|---|---|
| 8.    x | $x + y = 6$    y | 8._____ |

9.
```
   4,564            2,096
 -     y          -     z
   2,096            4,564
       y                z
```
9._____

10.   243,000        $2.43 \times 100{,}000$    10._____

11. 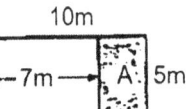        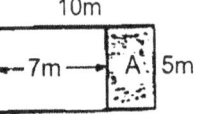    11._____

Each region is rectangular

The area of shaded region A      The area of shaded region B

12.   $\$10{,}428 \div 2$        $\$521.40$    12._____

13.   An odd number less than 5        An even number less than 10    13._____

14. 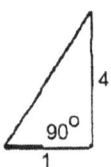        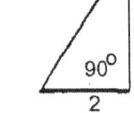    14._____

     Area of this triangle        Area of this triangle

15.   $\dfrac{9}{8} \div \dfrac{3}{8}$        $\dfrac{9}{8} \times \dfrac{8}{3}$    15._____

16. 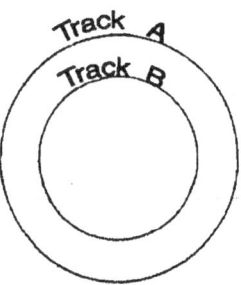    16._____

Car A circles Track A in 10 seconds.
Car B circles Track B in 10 seconds.

Car A's average speed        Car B's average speed
in kilometers per hour        in kilometers per hour

3 (#6)

| COLUMN A | COLUMN B | |
|---|---|---|
| 17. $3.00 | The simple interest earned on $100 for 6 months if the rate is 6% per year | 17._____ |
| 18. The number of whole numbers between 4 and 10 | The number of fractions between 1 and 2 | 18._____ |

19.

| The ratio of stars to circles after 400 stars and 200 circles are added to those above | The ratio of stars to circles after 50 stars and 25 circles are added to those above | 19._____ |
|---|---|---|
| 20. $\frac{x}{3}+\frac{x}{3}+\frac{x}{3}=3$ <br> x | $\frac{y}{4}+\frac{y}{4}+\frac{y}{4}+\frac{y}{4}=4$ <br> y | 20._____ |
| 21. The remainder when M is divided by 5 | The last digit of M is 2. <br> The last digit of N is 3. <br> The remainder when N is divided by 5 | 21._____ |
| 22. The average of 10, 20, and 30 | The average of 5, 10, and x, if x is a number greater than 30 | 22._____ |

23.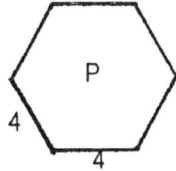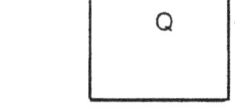

| The area of regular hexagon P | The area of square Q | 23._____ |
|---|---|---|
| 24. An area of 100 square centimeters | An area of 1 square meter | 24._____ |

25.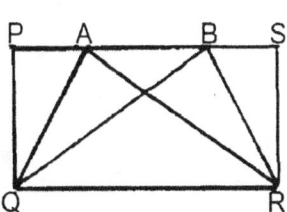

Rectangle PQRS

| Perimeter △ AQR | Perimeter △ BQR | 25._____ |
|---|---|---|

125

# KEY (CORRECT ANSWERS)

1. C
2. C
3. A
4. B
5. D

6. A
7. A
8. D
9. C
10. C

11. B
12. A
13. D
14. C
15. C

16. A
17. C
18. B
19. C
20. B

21. B
22. D
23. A
24. B
25. D

# DATA SUFFICIENCY

To further extend and measure the mathematical or quantitative ability of the candidate, a novel item, the test of data sufficiency, has been added to the mathematical aptitude section of the examination.

The candidate is presented with a problem for which two (2) facts (statements) are given. Then, he is to evaluate, without *necessarily* solving the problem, the relevance or irrelevance of the relationship of each or both of the statements to the actual solution of the problem. The directions for choice of decision in this matter are five (5) in number and are fundamentally more intricate and complicated than the actual solutions and/or comprehension of the problem.

The problems themselves are fairly simple in nature, alternating between arithmetical and algebraic foundations. Note that it is *NOT* the solution itself that is sought here but, rather, an indication by the candidate that he knows how to proceed to solve the problem. That is, a show of problem-solving technique rather than of computational skill is the desired outcome in this case. The basis is apparently the attempt to essay the ability of the candidate to think and to outline directions of procedure on his own.

The directions and sample questions with answers that follow serve to definitively delimn this question-type. In addition, six (6) Tests of Data Sufficiency, consisting of sixty (60) quest ions, together with solutions, are presented to challenge the candidate and to assure his overlearning of this novel question-type.

## SAMPLE QUESTIONS AND ANSWERS

DIRECTIONS: Each of the questions below is followed by two statements, labeled (1) and (2), in which certain data are given. In these questions you do not actually have to compute an answer, but rather you have to decide whether the data given in the statements are *sufficient* for answering the question. Using the data given in the statements *plus* your knowledge of mathematics and everyday facts (such as the number of days in July), you are to blacken the box on the answer sheet under

- A. if statement (1) *ALONE* is sufficient but statement (2) alone is not sufficient to answer the question asked,
- B. if statement (2) *ALONE* is sufficient but statement (1) alone is not sufficient to answer the question asked,
- C. if *BOTH* statements (1) and (2) *TOGETHER* are sufficient to answer the question asked, but *NEITHER* statement *ALONE* is sufficient,
- D. if *EACH* statement is sufficient by itself to answer the question asked,
- E. if statements (1) and (2) *TOGETHER* are *NOT* sufficient to answer the question asked and additional data specific to the problem are needed.

1. In a four-volume work, what is the weight of the third volume?

    2. The four-volume work weighs 8 pounds.
    3. The first three volumes together weigh 6 pounds.

### EXPLANATION

From and (2), it is apparent that the fourth volume weighs 2 lbs. However, there is insufficient information to determine the weight of any of the first three volumes. Thus, the answer is E.

127

2. Pump Q takes how many minutes longer than pump P to remove all the water from tank T?
   1. Working together, pump P and pump Q can remove all the water from tank T in 16 minutes.
   2. Pump P can remove all the water from tank T in 25 minutes.

### EXPLANATION

From (2), we can determine only the rate of removal for pump P.
From (1), we can determine only the rate of removal of both pumps working together.
Using both (1) and (2), then, we can determine the relative rates of P and Q.
Thus, the answer is C.

3. Is X greater than Y?
   1. $3X = 2K$, $4Y - 3K$, K is positive.
   2. $X + Y = 5$

### EXPLANATION

From (1), $X = 2/3K$ and $Y = 3/4K$. Therefore, X is less than Y. From (2), the relative size of X and Y cannot be determined. Thus, the answer is A.

4. What is the size of angle P in △ PQR?
   (1) PQ = PR
   (2) Angle Q = 40°

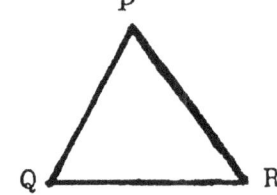

### EXPLANATION

Since PQ = PR from (1), PQR is isosceles. Therefore $\angle Q = \angle R$.

Since $\angle Q - 40°$ from (2), $\angle R = 40°$. Since the sum of the angles of a triangle is 180°, angle P can now be found. Since both (1) and (2) are needed, the answer is C.

5. What is the length of a certain cube's diagonal?
   1. The volume of the cube is 8.
   2. The diagonal of one face of the cube is $2\sqrt{2}$.

### EXPLANATION

From (1), each edge of the cube is 2. The square of the diagonal of a rectangular solid $= 1^2 + w^2 + h^2$. Since $1 = w = h = 2$, we can find the diagonal.
From (2), the side of the square face is 2. Again we have all the edges of the cube, and the diagonal can be found. Hence, the answer is D.

6. If x is a whole number, is x a two-digit number?
   1. $x^2$ is a three-digit number.
   2. 10x is a three-digit number.

### EXPLANATION

(1) is sufficient alone because the square root of any three-digit square of a whole number is a two-digit whole number.

(2) is sufficient alone because whenever a three-digit multiple of 10 is divided by 10, the result is a two-digit number.
Thus, the correct answer is D.

7. In △RST, is angle R greater than angle S?
   1. Angle T is somewhere between 50° and 65°.
   2. ∠P = ∠S

   ### EXPLANATION
   From (1) alone or (2) alone, we cannot determine the relative size of R and S.
   From both (1) and (2), S may vary from 50° to 60°, and T from 80° to 50°, respectively.
   Thus, the answer is E.

8. John may sell a certain candy bar at 5 cents or 6 cents. If he wants to sell at a single price, at which price would his total receipts be higher?
   1. He can sell twice as many bars at 5 cents as at 6 cents.
   2. He can sell 30 bars a day at 6 cents.

   ### EXPLANATION
   From (1), if he sells n bars at 6 cents each, his receipts would be 6n cents; but he would sell 2n bars at 5 cents each and his receipts would be 10n cents.
   Fact (2) alone does not indicate the receipts if he sells bars at 5 cents each.
   Thus, the problem can be done with (1) alone, and the answer is A.

9. Is the average price of 24 items greater than 15 cents?
   1. 1/2 of the items cost 20 cents per item.
   2. 1/3 of the items cost 20 cents per item.

   ### EXPLANATION
   By knowing only the cost of a fraction of the items, it is impossible in either case to determine the average price of all 24 items, or whether this average price is greater than 15 cents.
   Thus, the answer is E.

10. If R and S are points on line segment PQ and R lies between P and S, how long is RP + SQ?
    1. PQ = 8 inches
    2. RS = 1/4 PQ

    ### EXPLANATION
    From (1) alone or (2) alone the length of RP and SQ cannot be determined.
    Using both facts, RS = 1/4 PQ = 2 and RP + SQ = 6. Thus, the answer is C.

# EXAMINATION SECTION
# TEST 1

DIRECTIONS: See DIRECTIONS under Sample Questions and Answers on Page 1.

1. In triangle ABC, how many degrees are therein Angle A?   1._____

    1. AB = AC
    2. Angle B = 40 degrees

2. There are 12 pencils in a box. How many have *both* erasers and dull points?   2._____

    1. 9 have erasers
    2. 3 have dull points

3. How many hours will it take some boy scouts and some scout-masters to put up a tent?   3._____

    1. The boys can put it up in 4 hours alone and the scout-masters in 2 hours alone.
    2. There are 3 scout-masters and 5 boy scouts.

4. Find the area of parallelogram ABCD.   4._____

    1. AB = 12 inches
    2. AD = 20 inches

5. How many nickels does John have in his pocket?   5._____

    1. He has 52 cents in coins in his pocket.
    2. Only one of the coins in his pocket is a quarter.

6. Find the number of degrees in an exterior angle of a regular polygon.   6._____

    1. The apothegm of the polygon is 6 inches.
    2. The polygon has eight sides.

7. Write an equation of the straight line.   7._____

    1. The line passes through the point (2, 3).
    2. The line is perpendicular to the x-axis.

8. Find the radius of a circle.   8._____

    1. The area of the circle is 36 $\pi$.
    2. The circumference of the circle is 12 $\pi$.

9. How many degrees in a base angle of an isosceles triangle?   9._____

    1. The vertex angle contains 70°.
    2. The area of the triangle is 14 sq. in.

10. Are two triangles congruent?   10._____

    1. They have equal bases and equal altitudes drawn to these bases.
    2. The triangles are isosceles.

# SOLUTIONS TO TEST #1

1. Answer (C)
   From (1), angle B = angle C, but this is not enough to determine angle A.
   (2) alone is not enough to determine A.
   If we use (1) and (2) together, B and C are each 40 degrees, and A is determined.
   Thus, the answer is C.

2. Answer (E)
   Since the facts in (1) and (2) are not mutually exclusive, there is no way of determining how many pencils have both erasers and dull points. Thus, the answer is E.

3. Answer (A)
   Using (1) alone, we can determine how long it takes them all to put up the tent.
   If it takes x hours, we may then solve the equation, $x/4 + x/2 = 1$.

   The information in (2) is irrelevant to the time it takes the group working together.
   Hence, the correct answer is A.

4. Answer (E)
   Finding the area of a parallelogram requires knowing the base and altitude. Either AB or AD may be used as base, but the altitude cannot be determined from the information given. The answer is, therefore, E.

5. Answer (E)
   Statement (2) merely tells us that the remaining 27 cents may be in nickels, dimes, or pennies, but there is not enough information to determine how many nickels. The answer is E.

6. Answer (B)
   Statement (1) is irrelevant to finding the exterior angle.

   The sum of the exterior angles is $360°$. Hence, from (2), we can divide by 8 to determine each of the exterior angles.
   The answer is B.

7. Answer (C)
   From (2), we see that the line is vertical.
   From (1), we see that the abscissa of every point on the line is 2.
   Thus, its equation is $x = 2$ from both facts.
   The answer is C.

8. Answer (D)
   Using the formula, $A = \pi r^2$, we can determine r from (1).
   Using the formula, $C = 2 \pi r$, we can determine r from (2).
   Hence, the answer is D.

9. Answer (A).
   Statement (2) has no bearing on the size of the angles of the triangle. From statement (1), we can determine the number of degrees in both base angles and, then, divide by 2.
   The answer is A.

10. Answer (C)
    Statement (1) merely establishes that the triangles are equal in area. If, however, the triangles are isosceles, then they are also congruent. Thus, the answer is C.

# TEST 2

1. Find the value of x.

    1. x + y = 5
    2. x - y - 1

2. The tax rate is 3%. Find the property tax.

    1. Property is assessed at 70% of its true value.
    2. This property is assessed for $6000.

3. How far is A from C?

    1. A is 20 miles from B.
    2. B is 20 miles from C.

4. Two angles A and B are complementary. Find A.

    1. The ratio of A to B is 2:1.
    2. The difference of A and B is 30 degrees.

5. What are the dimensions of a rectangle?

    1. The perimeter is 14.
    2. The diagonal is 5.

6. How many pennies does a boy have?

    1. He has 47 cents in coins in his pocket.
    2. One of the coins in his pocket is a nickel.

7. Find three numbers.

    1. The three numbers are in the ratio 5:7:9.
    2. The middle number is equal to half the sum of the first and third numbers.

8. Find three consecutive even integers.

    1. Their sum is 66.
    2. The largest is 4 more than the smallest.

9. If 4x - 8y = 4, find the value of y.

    1. x - 2y = 0
    2. x = 5

10. In triangle RST, find angle R.

    1. $\dfrac{RS}{ST} = 1$
    2. $\dfrac{RS}{TR} = 1$

# SOLUTIONS TO TEST #2

1. **Answer (C)**
   The value of x cannot be determined from either (1) or (2) alone. By adding the two equations and solving the resulting equation, x can be found.
   Thus, the answer is C.

2. **Answer (B)**
   The information given in (1) is irrelevant to the problem.
   The tax can be determined from (2) by taking 3% of $6000.
   Thus, the answer is B.

3. **Answer (E)**
   The information in (1) and (2) gives us two sides of a triangle. This is not enough to determine the third side. Thus, the answer is E.

4. **Answer (D)**
   Using fact (1), we see that A = 2B; this equation solved with A + B = 90 will yield A.
   Using fact (2), we see that A - B - 30; this equation solved with A + B = 90 will yield A.
   Thus, the answer is D.

5. **Answer (C)**
   From (1), we see that 1 + w = 7.
   From (2), we see that $1^2 + w^2 = 25$.
   We can solve these equations together for 1 and w. Each, by itself, is not solvable.
   Thus, the answer is C.

6. **Answer (E)**
   Both facts together do not supply enough information to answer the question. The remaining 42 cents may be in pennies, dimes, nickels, or any combination of these. Thus the answer is E.

7. **Answer (E)**
   There are many possible sets of three numbers that satisfy condition (1). Fact (2) gives us no additional information since any three numbers satisfying condition (1) also satisfy condition (2). Thus, the answer is E.

8. **Answer (A)**
   Statement (2) says nothing more than the fact that the three even integers are consecutive.
   Fact (1) yields an equation which is solvable to yield all three numbers; i.e., denote the numbers by x, x + 2, x + 4 and let their sum be 66.
   Thus, the answer is A.

9. **Answer (B)**
   Fact (2) can be substituted in the original equation to yield y. Equation (1) is inconsistent with the original equation and, as a result, they have no common solution. Thus, the answer is B.

10. **Answer (C)**
    From (1) and (2), we see that RS = ST = TR and the triangle is, therefore, equilateral. Angle R is, then, 60°. Thus, the answer is C.

# TEST 3

1. There are 75 people in the town that attend either meeting X or meeting Y or both. How many attend each meeting?

    1. 30 people attend meeting X only.
    2. 45 people attend meeting Y.

2. In triangle RST, angle S is 90 and SR = ST. Find the area of triangle RST.

    1. SR = 5
    2. RT = $5\sqrt{2}$

3. How many degrees in each angle of a triangle?

    1. One of the angles is 30 degrees more than another.
    2. The triangle is a right triangle.

4. Find the height of a flagpole.

    1. The shadow of a yardstick is 6 ft. long.
    2. At the same time and place, the shadow of the flagpole is 54 ft. long.

5. Find the side of a square.

    1. The area of the square is 36 square inches.
    2. The square is equal in area to an equilateral triangle.

6. What is the relationship of the fathers of two girls?

    1. The girls are good friends.
    2. The girls are first cousins.

7. Find the area of a parallelogram.

    1. Two adjacent sides are 20 and 12.
    2. One angle is 60 degrees.

8. Is a parallelogram a rectangle?

    1. Its diagonals bisect each other.
    2. Its diagonals are equal.

9. A cylindrical glass 6 inches high is full of water. How many pints of water does it contain?

    1. A cubic foot of water weighs 62.5 pounds.
    2. The diameter of the glass is 4 inches.

10. The bases of an isosceles trapezoid are 6 and 10. Find its area.

    1. The diagonals of the trapezoid are each 9.
    2. The lower base angles are acute.

# SOLUTIONS TO TEST #3

1. Answer (E)
   The 30 people in (1) and the 45 people in (2) are not mutually exclusive. Any of the 45 people in (2) may also attend meeting X. Hence, we cannot determine the number of people attending each meeting. Thus, the answer is E.
2. Answer (D)
   This is a right, isosceles triangle. If we are given any one side, we can find the other sides and, therefore, the area of the triangle. Thus, the answer is D.
3. Answer (C)
   (1) or (2) by itself is insufficient to determine the angles. Call the angles x and x + 30. From (2), these add up to 90 degrees and can, thus, be determined. The answer is C.
4. Answer (C)
   The two facts in (1) and (2) produce similar triangles. By setting up a proportion of the corresponding sides, the height of the flagpole can be found. Thus, the answer is C.
5. Answer (A)
   From (1), the side of the square is the square root of the area and can thus be determined.
   (2) yields inadequate information to determine the square.
   Thus, the answer is A.
6. Answer (E)
   (1) gives no evidence of any relationship.
   (2) fixes no definite relationship of the fathers since the girls may be related through their mothers.
   Thus, the answer is E.
7. Answer (C)
   From (1), we cannot determine the altitude of the parallelogram, which is needed for the area.
   From (1) and (2) together, we can determine the altitude to either one of the sides, and thus calculate the area.
   The correct answer is, therefore, C.
8. Answer (B)
   (1) is true of all parallelograms.
   If (2) is true of a parallelogram, the figure is a rectangle. Thus, the answer is B.
9. Answer (B)
   We do not need (1) since we are finding only the volume of the water and not its weight.
   Fact (2) gives us the radius, which is needed to find the volume. Thus, the answer is B.
10. Answer (A)
    By using (1) and the values of the bases, we can determine the altitude of the trapezoid and, thereby, its area.
    Statement (2) has no particular bearing on the area. Thus, the answer is A.

# TEST 4

1. Find the height to which each end of a seesaw can rise.   1.____

    1. The seesaw is 14 feet long.
    2. The board is supported at its center by a block 4 feet high.

2. Find the speed of a locomotive.   2.____

    1. The drive wheels are each 50 inches in diameter.
    2. The wheels make 140 revolutions per minute.

3. John has 5 coins in his pocket. Does he have a quarter?   3.____

    1. He has 45 cents in his pocket.
    2. One of the coins is a nickel.

4. A table is 30 inches long and 9 inches wide. It is covered by three overlapping napkins, each 9 inches wide. How long is each of the napkins?   4.____

    1. All three napkins are of equal length.
    2. If the table were 1 1/2 times as long as it is now, the napkins would just cover the table without overlapping.

5. Find x and y   5.____

    1. $2x + y = 10$
    2. $3x - y = 15$

6. Is a quadrilateral a square?   6.____

    1. It is equilateral.
    2. The diagonals are perpendicular to each other.

7. G and S go on a 300-mile trip by car. They take turns driving, each driving for 8 hours. Find the average rate of each.   7.____

    1. G drove 48 miles more than S.
    2. G averaged 6 miles an hour faster than S.

8. Find the area of a trapezoid.   8.____

    1. The bases of the trapezoid are 8 and 12.
    2. One of the lower base angles is 45°.

9. The distance to Bill's house is 40 miles from his college. Bill went to school Friday but then returned home. How long did the entire trip take?   9.____

    1. If Bill went 40 miles per hour faster, it would have taken him half the time.
    2. He traveled at a uniform rate, both going and coming, of 40 miles per hour.

10. Can a salesman compute his earnings for the entire week?   10.____

    1. He knows his sales for each day of the week.
    2. He works on a commission basis, which is 10% of his total sales.

# SOLUTIONS TO TEST #4

1. Answer (B)
   It is not necessary to know statement (1).
   Fact (2) alone tells us that one end may rise to a height of 8 feet, since the support is at the center.
   Thus, the answer is B.

2. Answer (C)
   From (1), we can find the circumference of each drive wheel.
   Using (1) together with (2), we can find the distance traveled by each drive wheel per minute, thus giving the speed.
   The correct answer is, therefore, C.

3. Answer (E)
   (2) tells us that he has 4 coins besides the nickel.
   (1) tells us further that the 4 coins must add up to 40 cents. These might be 4 dimes. Hence, we cannot conclude that John definitely has a quarter. Thus, the correct answer is E.

4. Answer (C)
   Fact (1) alone does not determine each napkin since they may overlap. Using (2) as well, we see that 3 napkins of equal length would just cover a 45-inch table. Thus, the answer is C.

5. Answer (C)
   Neither equation by itself can determine x or y. However, the two equations can be solved simultaneously for x and y. The answer is C.

6. Answer (E)
   Both of these properties of a square are also the properties of a rhombus. Hence, there is not enough information here to determine whether the quadrilateral is a square. The answer is E.

7. Answer (D)
   Using (1) alone, we can determine the distances traveled by G and S. Since they each traveled 8 hours, their rates can be determined.
   Using (2) alone, let r = the rate of S and r+ 6 = the rate of G. Then $8r + 8(r + 6) = 300$, and r can be determined.
   Thus, the correct answer is D.

8. Answer (E)
   Since the trapezoid is not necessarily isosceles, we cannot determine its altitude from all the given information. (The area of a trapezoid equals half the altitude times the sum of the bases.) Hence, the area cannot be determined. The answer is E.

9. Answer (D)
   From (2), it is apparent that it would take Bill one hour to go each way, so that his total time is determined.
   Using (2), let r = Bill's original rate; then $(r + 40) = 80$, and r can be found, and, therefore, the time for the round trip. The correct answer is D.

10. Answer (C)
    From (1), he can determine his total sales for the week.
    From (2), he can take 10% of his total sales to determine his earnings.
    Thus, the correct answer is C.

# TEST 5

1. Is a trapezoid isosceles?

    1. One base is twice the other.
    2. The diagonals are equal.

2. Find the value of p.

    1. $p + q = 5$
    2. p and q are rational numbers.

3. What were Jim's marks on his last two tests?

    1. His average for the last three tests is 80%.
    2. He received 80% on his first test.

4. Find the area of a regular hexagon.

    1. One side is 8.
    2. The apothegm is $4\sqrt{3}$.

5. Is Florium the best toothpaste?

    1. It contains 10% iridium.
    2. Many professional baseball pitchers use Florium.

6. Is John a member of the Arista?

    1. John is a senior.
    2. Only seniors are eligible to join the Arista.

7. Are the diagonals of a parallelogram perpendicular to each other?

    1. The parallelogram is a rectangle.
    2. The parallelogram is equilateral.

8. Find the area of a right isosceles triangle.

    1. The hypotenuse of the triangle is 10 inches.
    2. The median to the hypotenuse is equal to half the hypotenuse.

9. Two cars are traveling toward each other on the same highway. In how many hours will they meet?

    1. They are now 217 miles apart.
    2. One is traveling *at* 27 miles per hour and the other at 35 miles per hour.

10. At what time will the passenger train overtake the freight train?

    1. An eastbound freight train left Buffalo traveling at the rate of 40 miles per hour.
    2. Two hours later, an eastbound passenger train left the same station, traveling 60 miles per hour.

# SOLUTIONS TO TEST #5

1. Answer (B)
   (1) has no bearing on whether the trapezoid is isosceles.
   (2) alone is sufficient to establish that the trapezoid is isosceles. Thus, the answer is B.
2. Answer (E)
   The values of p and q cannot be determined from (1) and (2) or both. Thus, the correct answer is E.
3. Answer (E)
   From both (1) and (2), we can determine that the average of the last two tests was 80%. However, this is not sufficient to determine the grade on each test. The correct answer is E.
4. Answer (D)
   The side of a regular hexagon forms with two of its radii an equilateral triangle. Hence, from (1) we can determine the apothegm. Likewise, from (2), we can reverse the process and find the side. Since the area of the hexagon is six times the area of the triangle, it is determined by (1) or (2). Thus, the correct answer is D.
5. Answer (E)
   From the information in (1), we have no idea what effect iridium has on the teeth.
   The fact in (2), that pitchers use Florium, has no bearing on its quality as a toothpaste.
   The correct answer is E.
6. Answer (E)
   Both (1) and (2) together do not determine whether John is a member of the Arista.
   Thus, the answer is E.
7. Answer (B)
   From (1), the diagonals of a rectangle need not be perpendicular. From (2), the figure is a rhombus whose diagonals are perpendicular. Thus, the answer is B.
8. Answer (A)
   From (1), each leg of the triangle can be determined by the Pythagorean Theorem. Thus the area can be obtained.
   Fact (2) is true of all right triangles and has no bearing on determining the area.
   The correct answer is A.
9. Answer (C)
   (1) alone indicates the distance between them but does not state how fast they are approaching each other.
   (2) alone indicates the rate of approach but fails to state the distance apart. Using both (1) and (2), let t = the number of hours it takes them to meet; then, the equation $27t + 35t = 217$ leads to the desired result.
   The answer is C.
10. Answer (E)
    From all the given information, it is possible to determine how long it will take for the passenger train to overtake the freight train. If it takes t hours, we may solve the equation, $60t = 40(t + 2)$. However, we do not know at what time either train started and, therefore, we cannot answer the desired question.
    Hence, the correct answer is E.

# TEST 6

1. Find the height of a tree.                                                                1._____

    1. At 10 A.M., the tree casts a shadow 35 feet long.
    2. At the same time and place, a yardstick casts a shadow 2 feet long.

2. The circumference of circle P is how many times that of circle Q?                         2._____

    1. The diameter of circle P is twice that of circle Q.
    2. The area of circle P is 4 times that of circle Q.

3. How many 2-cent stamps did a woman buy?                                                   3._____

    1. She spent 60 cents for stamps.
    2. Some of the stamps were 2-cent stamps and some were 3-cent stamps.

4. What is a boy's average speed for a round trip to school and back?                        4._____

    1. He rides to school at 30 mph and returns home at 20 mph.
    2. The distance from home to school is 10 miles.

5. Into how many right triangles can a rectangular sheet of paper be cut?                    5._____

    1. The sheet of paper is 6 inches by 8 inches.
    2. Each triangle is to be 2 square inches in area.

6. What is the original price of a book?                                                     6._____

    1. The book was sold for $3.80.
    2. A discount of 40% was granted on the sale.

7. In how many seconds will an armature turn through 360?                                    7._____

    1. The armature is 4 inches in diameter.
    2. The armature turns at 120 revolutions per minute.

8. How many boys in the senior class?                                                        8._____

    1. There are 140 pupils in the class.
    2. The ratio of boys to girls is 4:3.

9. Find the area of an equilateral triangle.                                                 9._____

    1. A side of the triangle is 10.
    2. An altitude of the triangle is $5\sqrt{3}$.

10. Find each angle of a triangle.                                                           10._____

    1. The triangle is scalene.
    2. The three angles of the triangle are in the ratio 2:5:8.

---

141

# SOLUTIONS TO TEST #6

1. Answer (C)
   Using both facts (1) and (2), we can set up similar triangles that will permit us to solve for the height of the tree. Thus, the answer is C.

2. Answer (D)
   From the formula C = 2πr, we can find C when given r. From (1), r = 1/2 of the diameter. From (2), we can obtain r from the formula, $A = \pi r^2$
   Hence, we can use either (1) or (2). The answer is D.

3. Answer (E)
   Using statements (1) and (2), there are many possible answers to the equation that is formed, 2x + 3y = 60. To get a unique solution, we would have to know the total number of stamps purchased. The answer is E.

4. Answer (A)
   The average speed can be computed from (1) alone.
   The datum in (2) is irrelevant. Choose any distance from home to school, and the average rate will be the same.
   The answer is A.

5. Answer (C)
   Using both (1) and (2), the sheet can be cut into rectangles, each 4 sq. in. in area. Each of these rectangles can then be cut into 2 right triangles. The answer is C.

6. Answer (C)
   From statement (2), the book was sold for 60% of its original price. From (1), form the equation, 6x = 3.80, and solve to obtain the original price.
   Both (1) and (2) are needed.
   The answer is C.

7. Answer (B)
   Statement (1) is irrelevant to the problem.
   From (2), we can see that the armature does 1 revolution in 1/2 minute. The answer is B.

8. Answer (C)
   From (2), we can designate the number of boys and girls as 4x and 3x, respectively.
   From (1), we can form the equation, 4x + 3x = 140.
   Both facts are needed to obtain a solution.
   The answer is C.

9. Answer (D)
   From the formula, $A = \frac{s^2}{4}\sqrt{3}$ we can find the area from (1).
   Using (2) and the formula $h = \frac{s}{2}\sqrt{3}$, we can find s and then determine the area.
   Either (1) or (2) can, thus, be used. The answer is D.

10. Answer (B)
    (1) is irrelevant to finding the angles of the triangle. Using (2), form the equation, 2x + 5x + 8x = 180. Thus (2) is needed but not (1).
    The answer is B

# ANALYTICAL REASONING

## COMMENTARY

This unique type of question focuses on the ability to understand a structure of relationships and to draw conclusions about that structure. The examinee is asked to understand the conditions used to establish the structure of the relationship and to deduce new information from them. Each group of questions consists of (1) a set of several related conditions (and sometimes other explanatory material) describing a structure of relationships, and (2) three or more questions that test understanding of the implications of that structure. Although each question in a group is based on the same set of conditions, the questions are independent of one another; answering one question in a group does not depend on answering any other question.

Each group of questions is based on a set of conditions that establish relationships among persons, places, things, or events. The relationships are common ones such as temporal order

> (A arrived before B but after C);spatial order
> (X always sits in front of Y and behind Z);
> group membership (If Professor Smith serves on
> the committee, then Professor Jones must also
> serve); and family structure (Jane is John's
> mother and Beth's sister).

The conditions should be read carefully to determine the exact nature of the relationships involved. Some relationships are fixed (J and K always sit at the same table). Other relationships are variable (S must be assigned to either table 1 or table 3). Some relationships that are not stated in the conditions can be deduced from those that are stated (if one condition about books on a shelf specifies that Book M is to the left of Book N, and another specifies that Book O is to the left of Book M then it can be deduced that Book O is to the left of Book N.)

No knowledge of formal logic is required for solving these problems. These questions are intended to be answered using knowledge, skills, and reasoning ability which are expected of college students and graduates.

SUGGESTED APPROACH

Some persons may prefer to answer first those questions in a group that seem to pose little difficulty and then to return to those that seem troublesome. It is best not to start one group before finishing another because much time can be lost in returning to a question group and reestablishing familiarity with its relationships. Do not assume that, because the conditions for a set look long or complicated, the questions based on those conditions will be especially difficult.

In reading the conditions, do not introduce unwarranted assumptions; for instance, in a set establishing relationships of height and weight among the members of a team, do not assume that a person who is taller than another person must weigh more than that person.

It is intended that the conditions be as clear as possible; do not interpret them as if they were designed to trick you. For example, if a question asks how many people could be eligible to serve on a committee, consider only those people named in the explanatory material unless directed otherwise. When in doubt, read the conditions in their most obvious sense. However, the language in the conditions is intended to be read for precise meaning. It is essential, for instance, to pay particular attention to words that describe or limit relationships, such as *only, exactly, never, always, must be, cannot be,* and the like. The result of the careful reading described above should be a clear picture of the structure of relationships involved, including what kinds of relationships are permitted, who or what the participants in the relationships are, and what is and is not known about the structure of the relationships. For instance, following a careful reading it can often be determined whether only a single configuration of relationships is permitted by the conditions or whether alternative configurations are permitted.

Each question should be considered separately from the other questions in its group; no information, except what is given in the original conditions, should be carried over from one question to another. In some cases a question will simply ask for conclusions to be drawn from the conditions as originally given. An individual question can, however, add information to the original conditions or temporarily suspend one of the original conditions for the purpose of that question only. For example, if Question 1 adds the information "if P is setting at table 2 ....," this information should NOT be carried over to any other question in the group.

Many people find it useful to underline key points in the conditions.

As the directions for this type of question suggest, it may prove very helpful to draw a diagram representing the configuration to assist you in answering the question.

Even though some people find diagrams to be very helpful, other people seldom use them. And among those who do regularly use diagrams in solving these problems, there is by no means universal agreement on which kind of diagram is best for which problem or in which cases a diagram is most useful. Therefore, do not be concerned if a particular problem in the test seems to be best approached without the use of diagrams.

# EXAMINATION SECTION
# TEST 1

DIRECTIONS: Each question or incomplete statement is followed by several suggested answers or completions. Select the one that BEST answers the question or completes the statement. *PRINT THE LETTER OF THE CORRECT ANSWER IN THE SPACE AT THE RIGHT.*

QUESTIONS 1-7.

Questions 1-7 refer to the following information:

Seven individuals attended a picnic at Majestic View Park. No two of these people are the same age. The following information is also known:
  I.   Jack's age is exactly one-third of Ken's age and Jack is younger than Paula.
  II.  Oliver is 8 years older than Paula.
  III. Laura's age plus Nancy's age equals Jack's age, but this sum is less than Mary's age.
  IV.  Ken's age is exactly double that of Paula's.
  V.   None of the seven individuals is younger than 10 years old nor older than 100 years old.
  VI.  Laura is not the youngest person.
  VII. Mary's age is the average of Paula's age and Ken's age.

1. The OLDEST person is

   A. Laura           B. Mary            C. Ken
   D. Nancy           E. none of these

2. The LOWEST age that Jack could be is

   A. 12              B. 15              C. 18
   D. 21              E. 24

3. The HIGHEST age that Oliver could be is

   A. 58              B. 62              C. 66
   D. 70              E. 74

4. The individual who is *older* than 3 people and also *younger* than 3 people is

   A. Laura           B. Mary            C. Oliver
   D. Jack            E. none of these

5. How many individuals are *older* than Mary?

   A. 0               B. 1               C. 2
   D. 3               E. 4

6. If Jack were 30 years old, then Paula could be

   A. 33                          B. 34
   C. 35                          D. any of the above
   E. none of the above

145

7. Which of the following *correctly* lists the individuals by age in *ascending* order?

    A. Laura, Nancy, Paula, Oliver, Jack, Mary, Ken
    B. Nancy, Jack, Paula, Laura, Oliver, Ken, Mary
    C. Laura, Jack, Nancy, Paula, Ken, Mary, Oliver
    D. Paula, Laura, Jack, Mary, Oliver, Ken, Nancy
    E. Nancy, Laura, Jack, Paula, Oliver, Mary, Ken

7.____

QUESTIONS 8-14.

Questions 8-14 refer to the following information.

Rose, Sue, Ted, Viola, and William went bowling at the Roll-E-Z Bowling Alley, where they each bowled one game. Although none of the bowlers revealed his/her score, the following is known:
    I. No two bowlers had the same bowling score.
    II. A female bowled the lowest score, and she bowled last.
    III. Ted did NOT bowl the highest score, and he bowled third in the order.
    IV. William bowled before Ted, and he (William) bowled a better score than two bowlers.
    V. Viola's bowling score was better than Ted's score, and she bowled after Sue but before Rose.
    VI. Sue bowled after William.
    VII. In conditions V and VI, the expressions "bowled after" and "bowled before" do NOT necessarily mean "bowled directly after" or "bowled directly before."

8. The *second* bowler in the order was

    A. Viola                          B. Sue
    C. either Sue or William          D. William
    E. Viola, Sue, or William

8.____

9. Rose bowled _____ in the order and scored _____.

    A. first; second best             B. next to Last; second lowest
    C. last; lowest                   D. last; second lowest
    E. first; best

9.____

10. The CORRECT listing of bowlers from *first* to *last* is

    A. Sue, William, Ted, Rose, Viola
    B. William, Viola, Ted, Rose, Sue
    C. Rose, William, Ted, Viola, Sue
    D. William, Sue, Ted, Viola, Rose
    E. Sue, Viola, Ted, Rose, William

10.____

11. Who bowled the highest score?

    A. William or Sue                 B. Sue or Viola
    C. William or Viola               D. Rose or Viola
    E. Rose or William

11.____

12. Ted's score was better than that of _____ other bowler(s).

    A. 1                  B. 3                  C. 4
    D. either 3 or 4      E. either 1 or 3

12.____

13. If Sue bowled better than Ted, which one(s) of the following is (are) necessarily TRUE?

    I. Sue bowled worse than Viola.
    II. Ted bowled worse than William.
    III. Viola bowled the best.

    A. I *only*
    B. II *only*
    C. III *only*
    D. *Exactly two* of the above
    E. All of the above

14. How many individuals bowled *after* William but *before* Sue?

    A. 0
    B. 1
    C. 2
    D. 0 or 1
    E. 1 or 2

QUESTIONS 15-25.

Questions 15-25 refer to the following information:

Amy, Bob, Carl, Donna, Ellen, and Florence are six individuals whose professions are: artist, bookkeeper, counselor, doctor, engineer, and fashion designer, though not necessarily in that order. They earn six different annual salaries, each one of which is a multiple of $5000. Also:

  I. The fashion designer is a female, but earns neither the lowest nor the highest salary.
  II. Carl and the engineer are bowling partners with the doctor, the latter of whom earns the highest salary. None of the other individuals bowl.
  III. The artist earned two degrees from State University, which she attended during the same time that Amy was attending that school. Currently the artist earns more than two of the other five people, including Donna.
  IV. Donna earns the least. Her steady boyfriend is the counselor, although she used to date the doctor.
  V. The fashion designer and the engineer were Ellen's guests at the latter's wedding reception recently.
  VI. The fashion designer earns more than the artist but less than the engineer.
  VII. Only the doctor earns more than Florence.
  VIII. The second highest income is $80,000 per year.
  IX. If the annual incomes were arranged in ascending order, the largest difference between any two consecutive salaries is $15,000.
  X. The fourth highest income is exactly double the lowest salary.
  XI. Each person's annual salary exceeds $25,000.
  XII. The second lowest income is exactly one-third of the highest income.

15. The artist is

    A. Amy
    B. Bob
    C. Carl
    D. Donna
    E. Ellen

16. _____ earned the HIGHEST salary and _____ earned the SECOND TO LOWEST salary.

    A. Bob; Carl
    B. Amy; Donna
    C. Ellen; Florence
    D. Bob; Ellen
    E. Amy; Florence

4 (#1)

17. Amy's annual salary is                                                                                              17._____

    A.  $60,000                                      B.  $65,000
    C.  between $65,000 and $80,000                  D.  between $60,000 and $80,000
    E.  between $60,000 and $75,000

18. The doctor's MINIMUM salary is                                                                                      18._____

    A.  $80,000              B.  $85,000                     C.  $90,000
    D.  $95,000              E.  none of these

19. _____ earns $40,000.                                                                                              19._____

    A.  Bob                  B.  Carl                        C.  Ellen
    D.  Donna                E.  none of these

20. The dollar difference between the counselor's and the artist's salary is                                            20._____

    A.  $10,000              B.  $15,000                     C.  $20,000
    D.  $25,000              E.  none of these

21. The individual whose salary CANNOT be determined exactly is the                                                     21._____

    A.  bookkeeper           B.  doctor                      C.  fashion designer
    D.  engineer             E.  artist

22. Donna is the                                                                                                        22._____

    A.  artist               B.  bookkeeper                  C.  counselor
    D.  engineer             E.  none of these

23. The engineer earns more than _____ individual(s).                                                                 23._____

    A.  0                    B.  1                           C.  2
    D.  3                    E.  4

24. The individuals who do NOT bowl are                                                                                 24._____

    A.  Donna, Bob, Florence                         B.  Donna, Bob, Ellen
    C.  Donna, Amy, Ellen                            D.  Amy, Bob, Florence
    E.  Amy, Florence, Donna

25. The CORRECT listing of the six individuals arranged from LOWEST salary to HIGHEST                                   25._____
    salary is

    A.  Ellen, Amy, Carl, Donna, Bob, Florence
    B.  Donna, Carl, Ellen, Amy, Florence, Bob
    C.  Amy, Ellen, Florence, Carl, Donna, Bob
    D.  Donna, Florence, Carl, Bob, Ellen, Amy
    E.  Ellen, Donna, Carl, Amy, Bob, Florence

## KEY (CORRECT ANSWERS)

1. C
2. D
3. A
4. E
5. B

6. E
7. E
8. B
9. C
10. D

11. B
12. E
13. B
14. A
15. E

16. A
17. D
18. B
19. E
20. D

21. C
22. B
23. E
24. C
25. B

---

# SOLUTIONS

For questions 1-7, let the ages corresponding to each person be represented by the first letter of the person's name (O for Oliver, for example). The seven conditions given yield the following equations: $J = 1/3K$, $J < P$, $O = P + 8$, $J < M$, $L + N = J$, $L + N < M$, $K = 2P$, $10 \leq$ each person $\leq 100$, $M = (P + K)/2$.

We recognize that Ken must be older than Jack and Paula. Also, since Jack is older than both Laura and Nancy, Ken is also older than Laura and Nancy. From the last equation, $M = (P + K)/2$, we know that Mary's age is between Paula's age and Ken's age; thus Ken is also older than Mary. Suppose Ken were younger than Oliver (i.e.: $K < O$). Since $K = 2P$ and $O = P + 8$, we would get $2P < P + 8$ r $P < 8$. This, however is not possible, since each person is at least 10 years old.

1. Self-explanatory from the above paragraph.
   (ANSWER C).

2. We determine that since $L + N = J$, Jack is older than both Laura and Nancy, but further analysis reveals that he is younger than the other four people. It is given that Laura is not the youngest; thus Nancy must be. Now, the lowest age for anyone is 10, and since no two people have the same age, if Nancy were 10, then the lowest age for Laura would be 11. Thus Jack would be 21.
   (ANSWER D).

3. If Ken (who is the oldest) were 100 years old, Paula would be 50. By condition II, Oliver would be 58.
   (ANSWER A).

4. We already know that $P < M < K$, from the statements $M = (P + K)/2$ and Ken is the oldest. We want to know if Oliver is younger than Mary. (By condition II, we know that Oliver is older than Paula.) If $O < M$, consider the fact that M is the average of P and K of P and 2P, which is $3P/2$. This implies that $O < 3P/2$. But $O = P + 8$. Thus $P + 8 < 3P/2$, implying that $P > 16$, which is certainly true. Had $O > M$, then $P < 16$, which is impossible since Paula is older than Jack and J 2:21. Thus Paula is the individual younger than 3 people.
   (ANSWER E).

5. Only Ken is older than Mary.
   (ANSWER B).

6. If $J = 30$, $K = 90$, then $P = \frac{1}{2} K = 45$.
   (ANSWER E).

7. Evident from information given in above explanations.
   (ANSWER E).

For 8-14 the following three matrices are possible. First letters of names are used.

Matrix 1

| Bowling Order | 1 | 2 | 3 | 4 | last |
|---|---|---|---|---|---|
| Score | | | | | |
| Lowest | | | | | R |
| 2 | | | T | | |
| 3 | W | | | | |
| 4 | | S | | | |
| Highest | | | | V | |

Matrix 2

| Bowling Order | 1 | 2 | 3 | 4 | last |
|---|---|---|---|---|---|
| Score | | | | | |
| Lowest | | | | | R |
| 2 | | S | | | |
| 3 | W | | | | |
| 4 | | | T | | |
| Highest | | | | V | |

Matrix 3

| Bowling Order | 1 | 2 | 3 | 4 | last |
|---|---|---|---|---|---|
| Score | | | | | |
| Lowest | | | | | R |
| 2 | | | T | | |
| 3 | W | | | | |
| 4 | | | | V | |
| Highest | | S | | | |

8. Only Sue could bowl second.
   (ANSWER B).

9. Rose will bowl last and score lowest.
   (ANSWER C).

10. Evident by reading the names from left to right in any of the three matrices.
    (ANSWER D).

11. Sue has the highest score in matrix 3; Viola is highest in matrices 1 and 2.
    (ANSWER B).

12. For matrix 1 or 3 Ted's score beat Rose's score, but in matrix 2, Ted scored second highest.
    (ANSWER E).

13. If Sue bowled better than Ted, then matrix 1 or 3 applies, and William bowled better than Ted. Matrix 3 does not support statements I and III.
    (ANSWER B).

14. If matrix 1 applies, the answer is 0. The answer is also 0 if matrix 2 or 3 applies.
    (ANSWER A).

For 15-25, the following matrix applies.

|  | Lowest | 5th | 4th | 3rd | 2nd | Highest |
|---|---|---|---|---|---|---|
| Salary | | | | | | |
| Profession | | | | | | |
| Artist | | | Ellen | | | |
| Bookkeeper | Donna | | | | | |
| Counselor | | Carl | | | | |
| Doctor | | | | | | Bob |
| Engineer | | | | | Florence | |
| Fashion Designer | | | | Amy | | |

15. Evident from the above matrix.
    (ANSWER E).

16. Evident from the above matrix.
    (ANSWER A).

17. Amy's salary is the 3rd highest and the 2nd highest is $80,000 by condition VIII. Now condition IX assures us that Amy's salary can be no lower than $65,000.
    (ANSWER D).

18. In the opening introductory paragraph for problems 15-25, we find that all salaries are multiples of $5000. Coupled with condition VIII, the minimum salary higher than 80,000 is 85,000.
    (ANSWER B).

19. By using conditions VII through XII, we can determine the following: Lowest salary = $30,000; 5th highest = $35,000; 4th highest = $60,000; 3rd highest = $65,000 or $70,000 or $75,000; 2nd highest = $80,000; highest = $105,000. Thus, no one earns $40,000.
    (ANSWER E).

20. The difference is $60,000 - $35,000 = $25,000.
    (ANSWER D).

21. The 3rd highest salary cannot be determined exactly, and this corresponds to the fashion designer.
    (ANSWER C).

22. Evident from the matrix.
    (ANSWER B).

23. Evident from the matrix.
    (ANSWER E).

24. From condition II, only Carl, the engineer (Florence), and the doctor (Bob) bowl.
    (ANSWER C).

25. Evident from the matrix.
    (ANSWER B).

# DEDUCTIVE REASONING

## 1. VALID AND INVALID ARGUMENTS

The recognition of valid or invalid arguments is largely a matter of experience and common sense. There are no universally valid approaches to such matters. Sometimes *Venn diagrams* can be useful.

Problem: Is this argument valid? All students in Mr. Thomas' class will be moving on to 6th grade next year. All students moving on to 6th grade next year will be going to the new school. Therefore, all students in Mr. Thomas' class will be going to the new school next year.

Solution: If you have trouble thinking through such reasoning, you might try drawing a Venn diagram like this one:

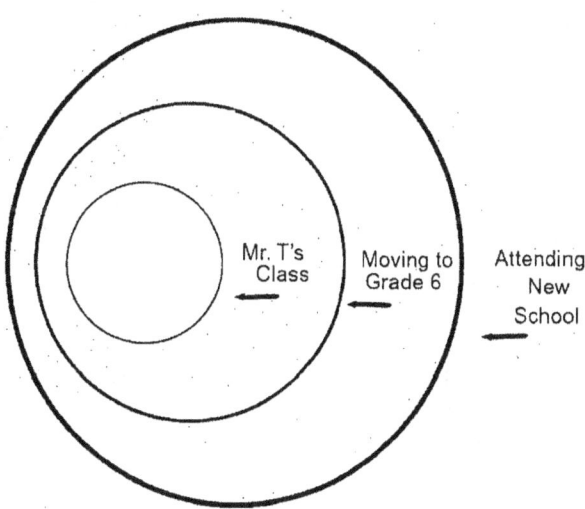

As you read through the original argument, you will see that the placement of the three circles reflects the relationships in the argument. Since all students in Mr. Thomas' class will be moving on to Grade 6, we put the circle of Mr. Thomas' students within the collection of all those moving on to Grade 6. And since all those going on to Grade 6 will be attending the new school, we put the Grade 6 circle within the circle of people going to the new school. You can also see by looking at the diagram that, indeed, all students in Mr. Thomas' class are within the new school circle. Thus all of his students will be going to the new school and the argument is valid.

Problem: If you have an average of 80% or better, then you are excused from taking the final exam. Lee was excused from taking the final exam. Therefore, Lee had an average of 80% or better. Is this reasoning valid?

Solution: No, it is not valid. You might discover the answer by thinking. It doesn't say that the only people excused from taking the final are those with an average of 80% or more. Maybe, for example, all seniors are also excused and Lee is a senior. Then Lee might have an average of less than 80% and still be excused from the exam. You might also draw a diagram.

153

2

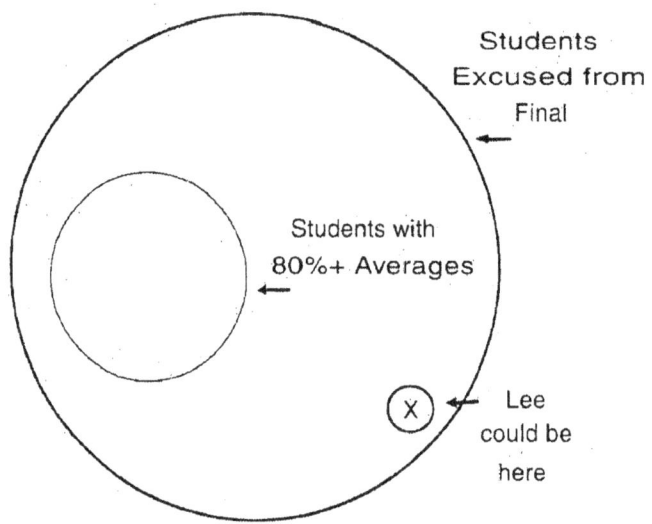

Problem: There are 30 students in Ms. Broso's English class. Twenty had a grade of C or better for the first marking period and 15 had a C or better for the second marking period. What is the smallest number of students who could have a C or better average for both marking periods?

Solution: You couldn't have the situation below where the two groups have no members in common because then you would have at least 35 students in the class and Ms. Broso has only 30 students.

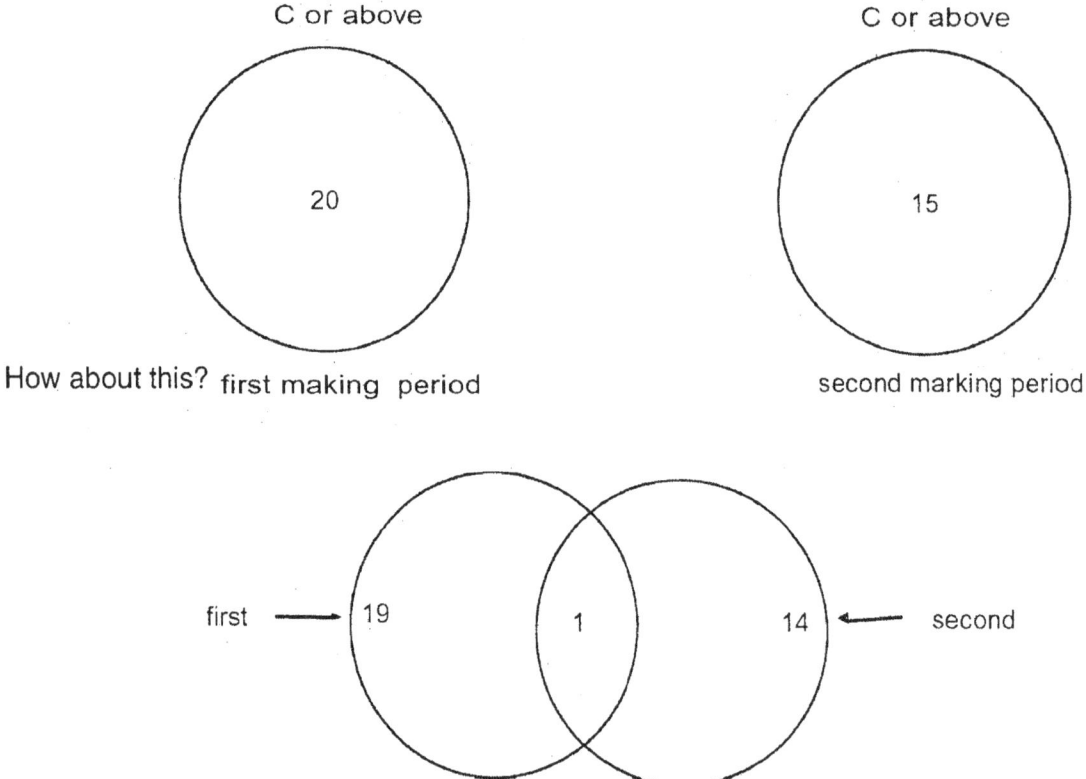

154

In this case, only 1 student had a grade of C or better during both marking periods. The total number of students is 34; the class size is still too large.

Finally, we realize that if 5 students have C's or better during both marking periods, we get

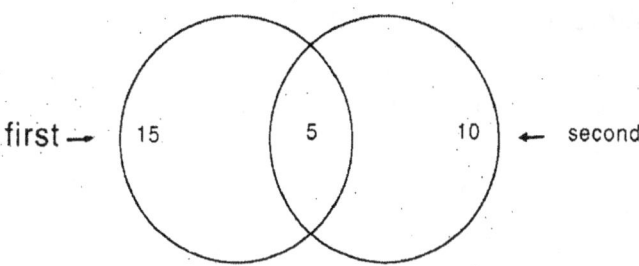

for a total of 30 students. Thus, if Ms. Broso has 30 students, at least 5 must have had C's or better for both marking periods.

Exercises

1. Identify the following summary statements as valid or invalid.

   a. All students who completed English 1 with a passing grade are eligible for English 2. Monroe is eligible for English 2. Therefore, Monroe completed English 1 with a passing grade.
   b. All animals that inhabit the savannah are plant eaters. All plant eaters in the savannah are nocturnal. Therefore, all animals who inhabit the savannah are nocturnal.
   c. If you complete English 2, then you must have written an article for the student newspaper. Sue has never written an article for the student newspaper so we know that she has not completed English 2.
   d. All freshmen are required to take physical education. Some students who take physical education score over 80 points on a physical agility test. Therefore, some freshmen score over 80 points on the physical agility test.
   e. Last year 80% of the children in Mr. Cruz's class passed the mastery skills test in mathematics. This year 85% of his students passed the test. Therefore, more of his students passed the mastery test this year than last year.
   f. All students who pass the placement test must take French 2. Some students who take French 2 later take French 3. Therefore, some students who pass the placement test later take French 3.
   g. All high school students like loud music. Therefore, if you're not a high school student, you don't like loud music.
   h. *If you have less than ten years teaching experience, you must fill out lines (b) or (c), whichever applies.* Martha did not fill out line (c). Therefore, she has more than ten years teaching experience.

2. Racebrook School enrolls 46 third grade students, of whom 93% passed the statewide mastery skills test in mathematics. In the state as a whole, therefore, on the third grade mastery skills math test,

A. about 93% passed
B. not everybody passed
C. the passing rate was 93% or less
D. rural schools' scores were less than suburban schools' scores

3. In a fifth grade class, 3/4 of the students have arithmetic skills above grade level and 3/4 have reading skills above grade level. Therefore,

   a. 3/4 have above-grade level skills in both arithmetic and reading
   b. 1/4 have above-grade level skills in both arithmetic and reading
   c. 1/2 or less have above-grade level skills in both arithmetic and reading
   d. 1/2 or more have above grade level skills in both arithmetic and reading

## 2. HIDDEN ASSUMPTIONS IN STATEMENTS

Most of us commonly encounter statements involving *hidden* assumptions, even though we are not routinely expected to make explicit what those assumptions are. Everyone is familiar with advertising pitches such as, *Test drive a Turtle today! America's most popular car!* This advertisement assumes that just because most people buy Turtles, so should you. (The assumption may well not be valid, however. Your own needs and desires may be very different from those of *most* Americans.)

*Clothing sale! 25% off selected items!* In this advertisement, the crucial word is *selected*. Maybe the owner has selected only a few items for this discount and most items are not on sale at all. In reading such an advertisement, you can certainly assume that not all items will be on sale, keeping in mind that most may not be!

Problem: A salesperson tells you, *None of our ovens come with less than a one-year warrantee.* You might reasonably conclude that
   a. most of the ovens have more than a one-year warrantee
   b. none of the ovens has a warrantee
   c. if you buy an oven from this salesperson, the warrantee period will be for one year or longer
   d. your oven will probably break down after 13 or 14 months of use

Solution: Choice (a) is incorrect since it might well be the case that all the ovens are warranteed for exactly one year. Choice (b) is incorrect because the salesperson's statement implies that all the ovens have warrantees. Choice (c) is correct because it is simply a rephrasing of the salesperson's comment. Choice (d) may offer a true statement but it does not follow from the salesperson's remarks.

Exercises

4. The sign reads, *All students with placement test scores of less than 60% should report to room 216 before signing up for Math 210.* Based on this information, you might reasonably conclude that

   a. a student with less than 60% on the placement test will not be allowed to take Math 210
   b. 60% or more is a good placement test score

c. most students with placement test scores of 60% or more do not need to report to room 216
d. some students scored 60% on the placement test

5. Read each of the following statements. In each case, identify one reasonable assumption underlying the statement.

   a. Our new super-low credit card interest rate is guaranteed until December 31!
   b. Save up to 50% on many items from one of New England's largest collections of gourmet cookware.
   c. If you would like me to give you some extra help on that chapter, go to room 216 right after school.
   d. It will take 3 days at most for us to approve your loan application.
   e. All items are $5 and up on this shelf.

6. *Three out of five doctors recommend Pusanol as a pain reliever.* A consumer who reads this advertisement should assume that

   a. if there are 50,000 doctors in the country, then 30,000 of them recommend Pusanol
   b. Pusanol is probably better than the other available pain relievers
   c. somewhere there are at least 3 doctors who feel that Pusanol is the best pain reliever
   d. someone interviewed at least 5 doctors and found at least 3 who were willing to recommend Pusanol

7. *Give this test to your algebra students. If they don't do as well as our students, then you should order our textbook: ROTE ALGEBRA.* A teacher not using ROTE ALGEBRA gives the publisher's test to her students. Her class averages 12 correct put of 28. The publisher claims that *students who use our text average 19 correct.* Identify which statements below , the teacher might reasonably assume based on this information.

   a. If her students had used ROTE ALGEBRA, they, too, would have averaged about 19 correct.
   b. It is better to have a higher, rather than a lower, average on the publisher's test.
   c. All classes which used ROTE ALGEBRA averaged 19 correct.
   d. A class averaging 20 on the test knows more algebra than a class averaging 12.

8. What are some assumptions made in the following statements?

   a. If you received an A in French I, then you may sign up for French II without taking the French Placement Test.
   b. Maybe Hilltop Academy is the place for your child. Over 80% of our seniors go on to college.
   c. I know he made that spoon bend solely by the power of his mind! Two physicists saw the spoon bend, and even they could not explain how he did it.
   d. You should be eating Puffballos for breakfast. Bob Bovine ate them when he was your age and today he is the National League's batting champion.

   3. GENERALIZATIONS AND COUNTEREXAMPLES

A generalization occurs when someone examines particular examples or cases and then gives a general rule which applies to the particular cases. For example, you might look at the equalities

$$1 + 3 = 4$$
$$1 + 3 + 5 = 9$$
$$1 + 3 + 5 + 7 = 16$$

and make the generalization, *The sum of consecutive odd integers, starting with 1, is a perfect square.*

You might reflect on student writing assignments you have graded over the past few weeks and make the generalization, *On a given assignment, the first papers I grade tend to get lower marks than the last ones I grade.*

Counterexamples are examples which show that generalizations are false. Thus one person might say, *If x is a number, then $x^2$ is always larger than x.* A second might respond, *You are wrong because I have a counterexample. Let x = 1/2. Then $x^2$ =1/4 and 1/4 is less than 1/2, so $x^2$ is not always larger than x.*

Problem: What counterexamples would disprove these statements?
  a. All fire engines are red.
  b. All American Presidents were born east of the Mississippi River.

Solution: a. Find a fire engine that is not red.
  b. Find an American President who was not born east of the Mississippi River.

Notice that the statements of Problems (a) and (b) both have the same form: *All A's are B's*. These are called universal statements, which always have negations of the form, *Some A's are not B's* or *There is an A that is not a B*. Thus to show that a universal statement like *All swans are white* is false, you need to show that *There is a swan which is not white*. A black swan would be a counterexample.

Problem: What counterexamples would disprove these statements?
  a. If it's made of glass, then this hammer can smash it.
  b. If $x^2 = y^2$, then x = y.

Solution: Notice that the statements of Problems (a) and (b) both have the same form: *If A then B*. These are called conditional statements, which always have negations of the form, *A and not B*. Thus to provide a counterexample for a conditional statement, you need something which makes A true and makes B false, in this case, something which is made of glass but which the hammer cannot smash or two numbers whose squares are equal but which are not themselves equal (e.g., when x = -3 and y = 3).

Problem: What would comprise a counterexample for the following:
  a. All horses have four legs.
  b. If you live in Connecticut, then you live in New Haven.

Solution:  a. A horse which does not have four legs.
b. A person who lives in Connecticut but does not live in New Haven.

Exercises

9. State a generalization suggested by the equalities below.

$$3 \times 10 = 30$$
$$4 \times 10 = 40$$
$$26 \times 10 = 260$$
$$48 \times 10 = 480$$

10. State a generalization suggested by the data below

### DAILY HIGH TEMPERATURE

| Month/Day | Anchorage Alaska | Bismarck North Dakota |
|---|---|---|
| 3/1 | 35 | -5 |
| 3/2 | 40 | 0 |
| 3/3 | 45 | 5 |
| 3/4 | 39 | 20 |
| 3/5 | 46 | 25 |
| 3/6 | 45 | 32 |
| 3/7 | 43 | 38 |
| 3/8 | 42 | 27 |

11. Consider this statement: *All teenage girls like horses.* Which of the choices below is a counterexample for this universal statement?

    a. Dora is 23 years old and she likes horses.
    b. Shema is 15 years old and she dislikes animals of any kind.
    c. George is 13 and he loves horses.
    d. Luanne is 8 years old and she dislikes horses.

12. Consider this statement: *If a, b, c are odd integers, then a + b + c is divisible by 3.* Which of the following is a counterexample?

    a. $a = 3, b = 4, c = 5$
    b. $a = 3, b = 5, c = 7$
    c. $a = 2, b = 6, c = 4$
    d. $a = 5, b = 7, c = 11$

13. State a generalization suggested by the situations below.

    $123{,}486 \div 13 = 9498.92$ (rounded)
    $713{,}713 \div 13 = 54901$
    $486{,}721 \div 13 = 37440.08$ (rounded)
    $615{,}615 \div 13 = 47355$
    $502{,}719 \div 13 = 38670.69$ (rounded)
    $881{,}881 \div 13 = 67837$
    $408{,}804 \div 13 = 31446.46$ (rounded)

14. Describe a counterexample for each of the following.
    a. If you live in Stonington, then you like to eat fish.
    b. All high school graduates have read Shakespeare's play, HAMLET.
    c. If a is larger than b and if c is not 0, then ac is larger than bc.
    d. All quadrilaterals are rectangles.

# SOLUTIONS TO PROBLEMS

1. a. Invalid:

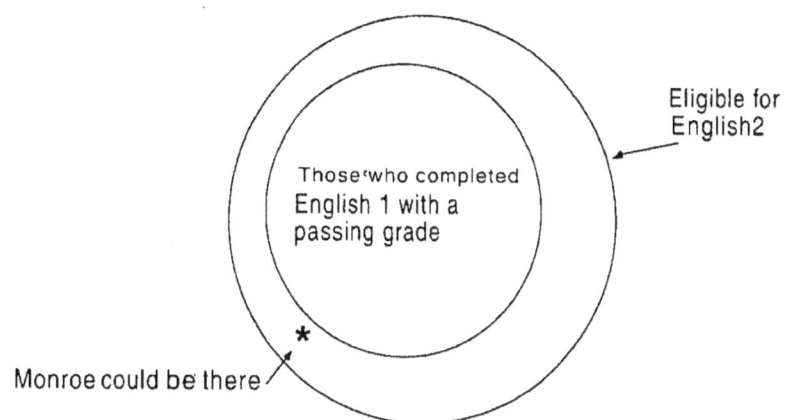

(To discover how wrong the argument is, consider this argument, which is identical in form: *All students who live in Hartford live in Connecticut. Monroe lives in Connecticut. Therefore, we know that Monroe lives in Hartford.*)

b. Valid:

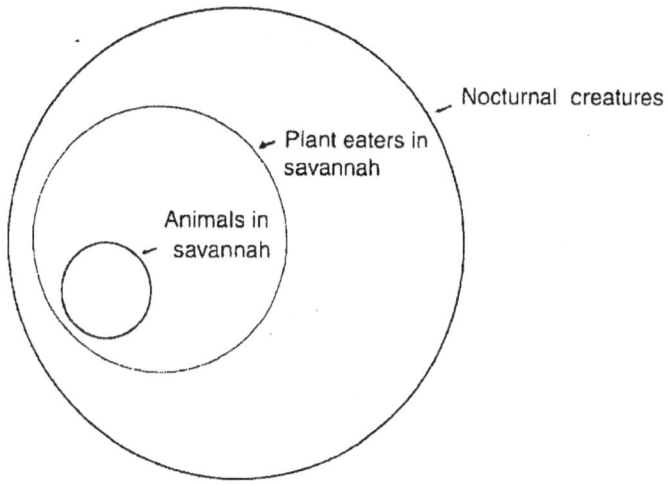

c. Valid:

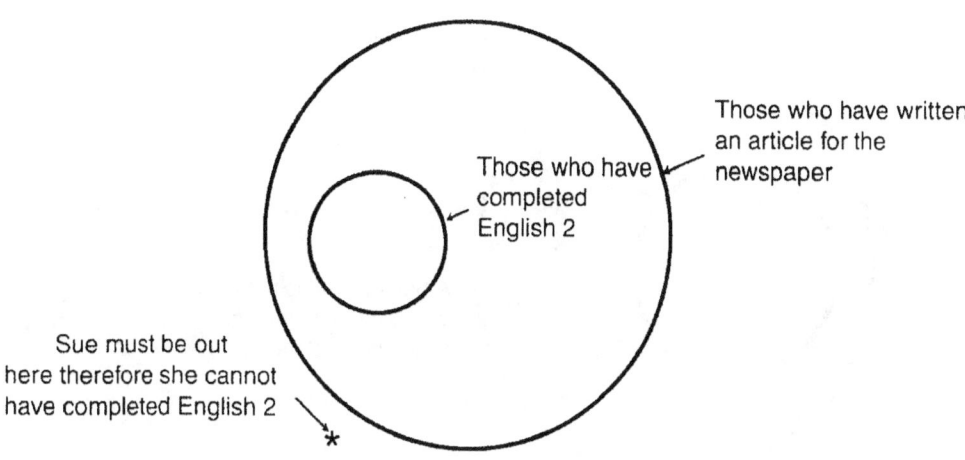

d. Invalid. The situation could look like this:

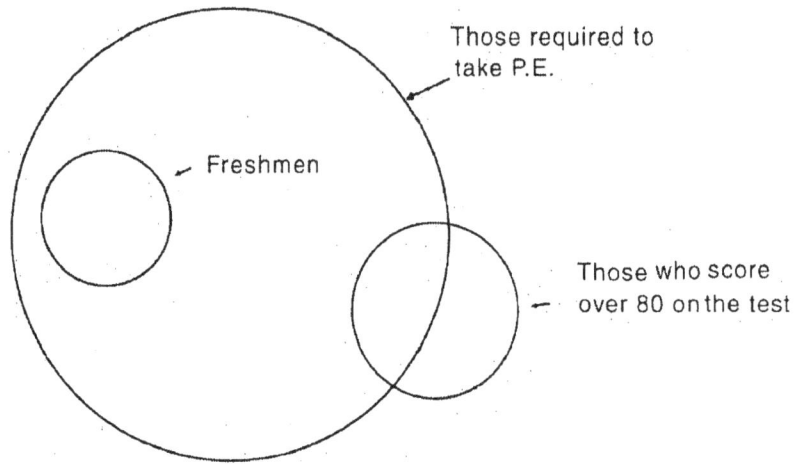

e. Invalid because the conclusion might be false. Maybe last year Mr. Cruz had 25 students. If 80% passed, then 20 students passed. (80% of 25 = .80 x 25 = 20). Maybe this year his class contained 20 students. If 85% passed, then 17 students passed. Thus it could happen that more students passed last year than passed this year.

f. Invalid. The situation could look like this:

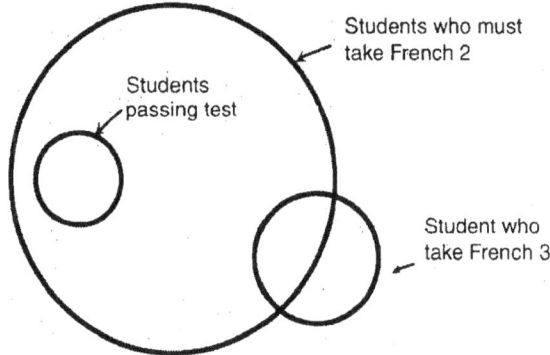

g. Invalid. Maybe this is the situation:

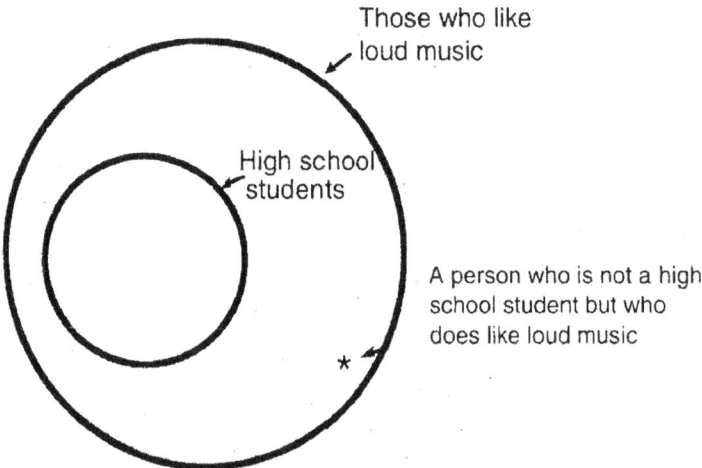

h. Invalid. Maybe she filled out line b instead.

2. We can be certain of only (b).

3. (d) is correct. The situation could vary from the case where: all who were above grade level in arithmetic were also above grade level in reading, to the case where: the two groups have minimal overlap:

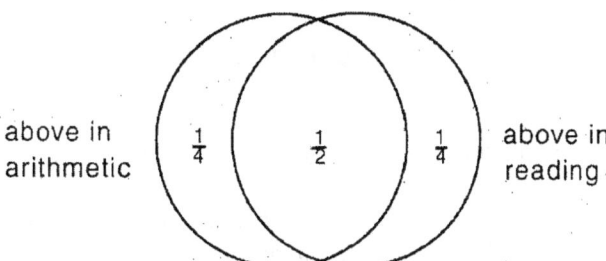

Here, 1/2 the students are above grade level on both tests, in arithmetic 1/4+1/2=3/4 of the students are above grade level and 1/4+1/2=3/4 of the students are above grade level in reading. You can't have any fewer than of the students above grade level on both tests. Suppose 40% were above grade level on both tests. The diagram would look like this:

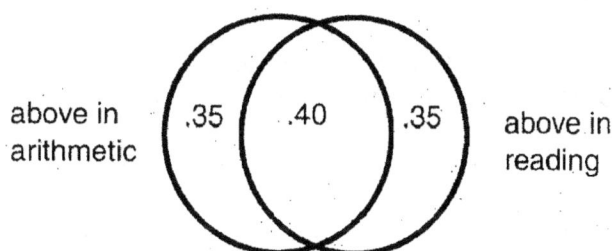

Then we have to put .35 in the other parts of the diagram because 3/4 (.75) of the students are above grade level in arithmetic and in reading. But now we have .35 + .40 + .35 = 1.10. This is too high! The fraction of students in the different areas must sum to 1. There is no way to do this if the center number is less than 1/2.

4. c

5. a. It may very well increase after December 31.
   b. The 50% savings will not be available on all (perhaps most) items.
   c. I will be in room 216 after school.
   d. The application could be ready in one or two days.
   e. Many items (perhaps most) will cost more than $5

6. d

7. No statements can be reasonably assumed.

8. a. If you received an A in French I and took the Placement Test, you would score well enough to enroll in French II.

b. It is meant for you to assume that the 80% figure was due to attendance at Hilltop. (If the group of students had not attended Hilltop, perhaps 90% of them would have attended college.)
c. It is assumed that physicists are especially equipped to judge the capabilities of spoon benders. (Magicians, for example, might make far better witnesses.)
d. It is meant for you to assume that Puffballos help create a batting champion. (Maybe Bovine would have done even better had he never eaten Puffballos.)

9. To multiply a whole number by 10, just add the numeral 0 to the end of the whole number.

10. The daily high temperature in Bismarck is always lower than in Anchorage.

11. The negation of *All A's and B's* is *Some A's are not B's*, In our case, the negation of *All teenage girls like horses* is *Some teenage girls do not like horses*. So for a counterexample we seek a teenage girl who does not like horses. Choice b is the answer.

12. The negation of *If A then B* is *A and not B*. In our case the negation is *a, b, c, are odd integers* and *a + b + c is not divisible by 3*. The correct choice, therefore, is d.

13. 13 will divide evenly into any six-digit integer where the digits repeat in groups of 3 (e.g., 713,713 or 881,881).

14.  a. *A and not B:* Find someone who lives in Stonington and does not like to eat fish.
   b. *Some A's are not B's:* Find some high school student or students who have not read HAMLET.
   c. *A and not B:* Find numbers a, b, c such that a is larger than b, c is not 0 and ac is not larger than bc.
   d. *Some A's are not B's:* Find or describe one or more quadrilaterals that are not rectangles.

www.ingramcontent.com/pod-product-compliance
Lightning Source LLC
Chambersburg PA
CBHW082044300426
44117CB00015B/2608